SUNDAY JOHN UDOH

SPIRITUAL PARENTING

UNDERSTANDING THE MISBEHAVIOUR IN CHILDREN

SPIRITUAL PARENTING
Understanding misbehavior in Children

ISBN 978-978-989-861-9

Published by
Sunday Udoh
Healthcare Rehabilitation and Research Initiative
P.O.Box 51441 Falomo-Ikoyi, Lagos-Nigeria.
healthresearch35@gmail.com
healthresearch35@yahoo.com
sjudoh@gmail.com
Tel.+2348063959781, +2348023029693

F&J PRINTING &PUBLICATION

Table of Contents

DEDICATION

Spiritual Parenting is an unavoidable assignments that carries lots of discipline from the side of godly parents in equipping themselves with spiritual balance diets in other for them to parents after the scriptural pattern.

Firstly, the dedication goes to who have been by divine arrangement parenting me as a parent in the Lord, Dr. & Mrs D. K. Olukoya, the General Overseer of Mountain of Fire and Miracles International.

Secondly, it goes to my lovely wife, Sister Alero A. Udoh in whom have been partnering with me in the spiritual parenting of the children God has given us: Grace, Anastasia, Abraham, Divine and Favour, you are all treasured by me.

ACKNOWLEDGMENT

My gratitude goes to: Dr. D.K Olukoya,General Overseer, MFM Worldwide,

- Pastor Ayo Ayeko, Coordinator, MFM Children Ministry Worldwide
- Pastor Isaac Makinde, Rector, MFM School of children Education and Christian Parenting
- Pastor(Dr) Emily Sydney, MFM Ministries Canada
- Evangelist Hazel Joyce Akpofe, Wales
- Sister, Helen Ufuoma Atigogo, MFM Ministries London
- Pastor Eyitayo Oluwalagba, MFM Ministries the Republic of Ireland Europe
- Bro. Joseph Abiodun Awolowo, U.S.A
- Bro. . Alex Osunde
- Sister, Kufre Ifeweckwu
- And to All Children Teachers

PREFACE

PREFACE

According to Psychology, Dr Riley, every child needs high support and high control. The quality of support and control they receive in life will greatly influence their personality formation. Controls are the disciplines and bounds we take a child through. Misbehavior is the tendency to act or make misguided attempts to meet a need that is not morally acceptable.

Behaviour is the actions and mannerisms made by individuals, organisms, systems, or artificial entities in conjunction with themselves or their environment, which includes the other systems or organisms around, as well as the physical environment.

THREE TYPES OF BEHAVIOUR

Some parents find it helpful to consider three general kinds of behaviour:

1. Some kinds of behaviour are wanted and approved. They might include doing of homeworks, being polite, and doing chores. These actions receive compliments freely and easily.

2. Other behaviour is not sanctioned but is tolerated under certain conditions, such as during times of illness (of a parent or a child) or stress (a relocation, for instance, or the birth of a new sibling). These kinds of behaviour might include not doing chores, regressive behaviour (such as baby talk), or being excessively self-centred.

3. Still other kinds of behaviour cannot and should not be tolerated or reinforced. They include actions that are harmful to the physical, emotional, or social well-being of the child, the family members, and others. They may interfere with the child's intellectual development. They may be forbidden by law, ethics, religion, or social norms. They might include very aggressive or destructive behaviour, overt racism or prejudice, stealing, truancy, smoking or substance abuse, school failure, or an intense sibling rivalry.

The family is a major contributor to the social vices happening all over the world. The breakdown of the family values and marriages contribute to the psychological misbehavior of the child and vices in our society. The family is also the agent of social development.

The family is the bedrock of any society; a strategic and divine institution, it is God's solution for the problems of humanity. Boyd D. Brooks *"Parenting is a daunting task, especially if you are young and inexperienced. Today, many parents find themselves disconnected from their children and overwhelmed with a sense of helplessness. There are two basic approaches to parenting that can be used- reactive parenting and responsive parenting".*

Spiritual Parenting is leadership, what is Leadership? Leadership is defined as the art of influencing of the behavior of individuals and groups spiritually towards a desired goal or Godly ways.

A leader knows the way, goes the way and shows the way to the children and people. As a vessel committed to child upbringing, you are a leader and or a teacher of children" or both.

1

THE RULE OF PARENTING I

- **Train up the child in the way of the Lord.**

Throughout Scripture, God is clear about the responsibility He has placed in the hands of parents. None is clearer than Deuteronomy 6::6-7, "*these commandments that I give you today are to be on your hearts. Impress them on your children. Talk about them when you sit at home and when you walk along the road, when you lie down and when you get up.*"

- **Look pleased to see them(Children)**

We want them to grow up to love and be loved, to follow their dreams, to find success. Mostly, though, we want them to be happy. But just how much control do we have over our children's happiness. The surest way to promote your child's lifelong emotional well-being is to help him/her feel connected to you. A connected childhood is the key to happiness.

- **Treat your Child with respect**

Lyle Perry "Respect your kids. Too many adults DEMAND

respect from kids without showing any respect in return, it doesn't work.

You show respect for your child when you:

a. Respect her/his feelings
b. Respect her/his opinions
c. Respect her/his privacy
d. Respect her/his temperament
e. Respect her/his body and personal space

- Enjoy their company

However, instead of worrying about how many minutes you can spend with your children each day, focus on turning those minutes into memorable moments. Parents often compensate for having such a small quantity of time by scheduling " quality time" of two hours at the Nature preserve. But the truth is that quality time may occur when you least expect it- yes.

Not every day with your children will be perfect, but hopefully one day you will greet their departure with a profound sense of satisfaction because you have given them what they need to feel like a successful parent.

- Parenting is not a competitive sport

Parenting should not feel like a competitive sport, it's pretty challenging without any added obstacles. Strive to be loving and kind, have the courage to ask for help to take a break when you need it, be kind to yourself, be yourself and strive to know more about parenting.

THE RULE OF PARENTING I

- **Teach them to think for themselves**

How to Raise Children who think for themselves?

In today's society, children are faced with many tough choices at a very young age. In order to help them learn to deal with potential pitfalls, parents must help kids learn to make good choices on their own. Though it may seem difficult, learning how to raise children who think for themselves can be done when you follow a few basic guidelines, and the payoff will be knowing that your children are well equipped with the skills they'll need to handle tough decisions.

Step 1.

Demonstrate with your own behavior how to make choices.

You can teach your children to think for themselves by showing them at every possible opportunity how you make decisions. Stand behind the choices you make, and express your reasons for making them, which will help them understand why you chose the way you did.

Step 2.

Allow your children time to play freely.

Unobstructed play is crucial to raising children to think for themselves and helpful for their development because it compels them to decide on what to play with and how. These first decisions are building blocks for independent thinking.

Step 3.

Give your children small choices.

Ask them to pick between 2 or 3 outfits, and whatever they choose, allow them to wear it. As you build up their confidence with these smaller decisions, ease them into larger choices, such as what to have for dinner, or ask for their input on where to go for vacation.

Step 4.

Avoid criticizing the choices your children make.

This is a form of second guessing and may make your children feel badly about their decisions. It may also cause them to feel insecure about the next decision they need to make.

Step 5.

Don't be quick to judge or arrive at a conclusion.

Refrain from making judgments or offering unsolicited opinions about situations your children find themselves in. If they hear your thoughts or advice, they may feel as if they need someone else to tell them what to think or feel. Instead, ask them what they think about the situation, and what they believe the choices are. Encourage them to talk about what decision they want to make and why.

Step 6.

Explain the rules that exist in your home or their school.

Helping them understand why the rules are in place will encourage children to decide to follow them.

Step 7.

Discipline your children when they make poor choices.

Make sure to keep your message short and simple. In 2 or 3 sentences only, inform them of which actions you are disappointed with and why, and what the consequences are. Use simple words whenever possible to make it easier for your children to concentrate on their actions.

Step 8.

Focus on the sin, not on the sinner.

Focus on the bad decision or behavior when disciplining, and not on the children themselves. Refrain from telling them they are bad, and use phrases like "your behavior is out of line" instead. This prevents children from feeling personally attacked, and helps them understand that it's their actions you are unhappy with, not them.

Step 9.

Follow through on discipline.

Your children need to learn that there are consequences for their actions and that making the wrong choice will lead to an appropriate punishment.

Step 10.

Refrain from threatening or bribing your children.

Using rewards or threats to influence their decisions will send a message that they are not capable of making good choices without external incentives.

Step 11.

Respect their right to decide on their own.

Trust your children, and respect their right to decide on their own. Once you have laid the groundwork, give them room to actually make choices, and do not interfere unless there is an imminent danger. They will make good and bad decisions along the way, but in order to get better at the process, they need to have the freedom to do so.

Whenever possible, take emotions out of your disciplinary tactics. Replace words such as "angry" with "disappointed." If necessary, avoid discussing bad choices with your children until you can speak calmly. If you address them with anger or outrage, they will likely focus their attention on your emotions rather than your actual message, which may make it easier to tune you out.

Make sure the punishment fits the crime. Overly severe punishments may have the opposite effect, causing your children to be angry with your actions rather than reflecting on their own. Whenever possible, discuss potential consequences for breaking rules ahead of time so there will be no mis communication later.

Warning

If it is within your control, never allow your children to make a bad choice when the consequences are life threatening. You need to step in as quickly as possible if they are making poor choices with regard to illegal activities, actions that put them in physical danger, or other choices with grave consequences.

USE PRAISE WISELY

Parenting & Praise

Raising your children may seem like such an obvious and -- all things considered -- easy part of parenting. Children love to be told how wonderful they are (who does not?) and how proud we are of them. When it comes to praise, there's more on the line than just boosting self-esteem. "A parent's job is to shape children's behavior," says Michelle Macias, MD, an associate professor of pediatrics at the Medical University of South Carolina, in Charleston, and a spokesperson for the American Academy of Pediatrics. "Children consider praise a reward in itself, and praise is a way to help them learn which kinds of behaviors are acceptable, even from the earliest days." In fact, Dr. Macias has a favorite piece of parenting advice that pertains to praise: "Catch them being good."

She recommends that parents say ten positive things to their children for every negative response. It is not that hard, and it does not have to be elaborate, says Dr. Macias, a specialist in developmental and behavioral pediatrics. She suggests that you comment on a behavior you like when you observe it. For example, when you notice your toddler entertaining herself with her blocks, simply say, "You're playing so nicely now." Here, recommended by experts, are six other ways of giving praise that will help your children become both confident and responsible.

Focus on Process, Not Outcome

A few years ago, the American Psychological Association (APA) published a report on a group of fifth-graders' reactions to solving math problems. Some children received praise for their intellect; others received praise for their hard work. The researchers found that praising children for their intelligence did more harm than good because it ultimately made them unable to handle failure. The children who received praise for their efforts, on the other hand, seemed to be more resilient and persistent. "Praising children for being smart is basically praising them for their given genetic endowments rather than for what they are trying to accomplish," says Shari Young Kuchenbecker, PhD, a psychologist and child development consultant in Los Angeles. "It is the love of the process, a positive attitude, and the desire to improve that makes children into 'can-do' kids," says Kuchenbecker, who is a spokesperson for the APA.

That is why she believes that when it comes to praising toddlers and preschoolers, it is essential to focus on the process rather than the result. For example, if your toddler loves to help you care for the family dog but sometimes makes a mess, say something like, "I know it's hard to carry the dog's water bowl without spilling, but I love the way you're trying." For your soccer-playing preschooler, try, "I like the way you follow the ball down the field." In both instances, you are praising the effort that leads to success, Kuchenbecker says, and when you do that, you can be positive even if the outcome is not ideal. It is okay to let them fail, she adds. "When we swoop in with our adult skills and do things for children that they can do for themselves, we undermine their sense of competence," says Kuchenbecker. Accomplishing tasks without adult help is crucial to a child's development of a good sense of self.

WAYS OF PRAISE

Look Them in the Eye

"How you give praise is as important or even more important than the words you use," says Mona, PhD, a psychologist in Los Angeles. "Use a warm, nurturing tone, and make eye contact," she says, "and when it's possible, get down to their level, face to face." This kind of interaction increases a young child's confidence.

Sarah Kearney, a Portland, Oregon, mom of three, uses this "in your face" technique often because of her 16 month old twins. "I always try to look directly at each child and use his or her name when I offer praise," she says. "I've been told that babies remember and comprehend more words when they hear their name, and looking the child in the eye helps me focus on him or her, which is especially important with the twins."

Choose Words Wisely

When it comes to praise, it is important to use appropriate language for your child's developmental stage. "To praise a baby, you might just coo at her when she smiles at you," says Leticia C. Lara, LCSW, a spokesperson for Zero to Three, the advocacy organization that focuses on the healthy development of infants and young children. As your children grow older, "use words that reflect their experience and that shows understanding and empathy," says Lara. For example, if your 2-year-old is determined to put on her own socks but cannot quite do it, say something like, "You're trying so hard to be a big girl and get those socks on. I can help you with that, and then you can slip your rain boots on by yourself."

Applaud Each Child's Individual Strengths

Children cannot help but compare themselves with others. When Kristine Dunne, noticed that her younger son, Rory, now 5, would often compare himself to his older brother, Jack, and fall short -- in everything from kicking the soccer ball to creating art projects -- she made an effort to offer extra encouragement to Rory. "I would acknowledge his gripes, point out that his brother had a head start, and then just move the focus," she says. For example, "Yes, Jack kicks the ball a long way, but I've noticed that you can run really fast." Experts say this approach helps children learn that everyone has strengths, and that they are all different.

COMPLIMENTS & PERSEVERANCE

Pay Attention to the Little Things

"Children thrive on attention, it makes them feel nurtured," says Lara. When Jill White, a mom of four from Reno, Nevada, notices that her 4-year-old son, Preston, has gotten himself ready for bed without being asked, she praises him in the form of extra books at bedtime. "On the one hand, I realize it's something he has to do," says White, "but it makes my night so much smoother when I don't have to nag him that I'm happy to reward him with a few extra minutes of reading." You can also boost your child's ego simply by commenting on or by describing what she is doing, which she will perceive as a form of praise, says Lara. For instance, "Thank you for brushing your teeth without being asked."

Don't Overdo It

"If you praise too much, you will lose credibility," says Kuchenbecker. "You can only say 'good job' or 'I love that picture' so many times before the words don't mean anything." Whenever possible, be specific. Say, "I love the way you colored every corner of that picture," or, "What a beautiful combination of colors you chose." Descriptive compliments like these give your child an idea of why he earned your approval. Make sure that the action merits praise; children can tell the difference between hollow praise and the real thing, says Kuchenbecker, and they do not need compliments for every little thing.

Commendation gives children the message that they are accepted and appreciated, experts agree, but over-praising -- "you're the best,""you're the smartest,""you're the most wonderful child" -- only sets them up for eventual disappointment. Some experts take it a step further and say that over-praising can make children feel pressured to perform and can develop in them the need to seek approval from others all the time. If you offer frequent encouragement, and save the praise for when it really counts, your child will be more resilient and confident because of it.

Keep Your Child's Chin Up

Have you ever made a remark that belittles your own abilities without thinking about the message you are sending to your children? "I'm a terrible cook," you might say to a friend in passing or, "I have no artistic talent." The next thing you know; your child is equally critical of herself/ himself. "The way to combat this with children is to acknowledge their frustrations but then offer hope and optimism,"says psychologist Mona. "If your child says, 'I can't draw a cat,' you might say, 'oh, that darn cat is so hard to draw. Let's try a moon now and a cat later.'" Or, if your preschooler is having trouble pedaling her tricycle, say, "Trikes are tricky! But if you keep trying, eventually you'll be able to do it."

Perseverance is key, agrees Shari Young Kuchenbecker, PhD, a psychologist and author of Raising Winners (Crown Random House). "When a child is trying something new, encouragement from you is both wonderful and essential," she says. For instance, when your preschooler is getting frustrated as she learns to tie her own shoes, you can watch and praise what she is doing right. "Good, that's how you cross those laces. I like the way you are sticking to it, even when it is hard to wrap that second place around the first. Your fingers will get stronger and will remember it better every time."

THE RULE OF PARENTING I

NEVER COMPARE CHILDREN WITH EACH OTHER

Comparison of children

Comparison is a common approach to ascertain the performance of your child. You compare your child's grades with others and then determine whether your kid's academic achievements are "normal", better or excellent. Then we resort to giving example of other children's accomplishment as a way to motivate our own child. "Learn something from other kids. Stop loitering in the neighborhood and join some classes". You certainly do not aim to hurt your child, but unknowingly these verbal statements do more harm than good. Comparing your child with others' is actually a way of putting some stress on you and your children and can be a useless activity, which the urge may be sometimes hard to resist.

Why You Should Stop Comparing Your Child with Others?
Negative Effects of Comparing Your Child
Positive Comparison Approach To Help Your Child
Parents and Peer Pressure

Why You Should Stop Comparing Your Child with Others?

Sometimes the sole motivation of comparing your child to others is to instigate competition in the child. So that this feeling can push the child to perform at par with his capabilities and excel. Competitiveness definitely is a driving force towards performance. But is this working for your child?

No two children are the same as they have different talents, interests, develop at different rates and have different strengths. Practically speaking, parents can either build or break the confidence and self- esteem of their child.

Expressing unhappiness due to poor performance or bragging about his achievements; both are appropriate. Read below to know about the negative effects of comparison and the alternative approach:

Negative Effects of Comparing Your Child

Stress: The child feels burdened if he is constantly battling with comparisons. Your job is not to pressurize him to perform and in turn making him anxious and insomniac. Sit and talk to your child, if there is something bothering him, which is affecting his performance. Devise solutions together.

Lowers self-esteem: The children start believing that others are better than him and that he is incapable of performing well or living up to the expectations of the parents. This feeling is very damaging for the personal and academic growth of the child.

Lowers self-worth: When in spite of his efforts, a child finds out that he needs to follow the other child to perform well, this breaks his confidence. The "good for nothing" starts to settle in and may deteriorate his performance further.

Shying away from Social Situations:
If your kid is consistently ridiculed or taunted by comparison,

then he will start avoiding public interaction with you.

Comparisons negative effects.

Builds a carefree attitude: If the child's talents or achievements are constantly ignored, then he may not even bother to please you anymore since you clearly favor the other child who has more "appropriate" achievements.

Suppresses talents.:

If your kid spends more time in charcoal painting, but you would have him go for badminton practice. The kid faces a dilemma. If the painting talent is unappreciated and he halfheartedly goes for playing badminton, he may not score very well. Eventually the painting talent would not have room to grow and will be lost.

Distances from you.

Clearly, if the kid is being held up negatively against his siblings, cousins, friends or neighbors. It becomes evident to him that something about him is unacceptable to you and you are unhappy with him. You become the source of hurt to him and he will try to maintain distance from you. This may make your kid feel insecure and lose trust in you and may lead to developmental or behavioral problems as your child matures.

Fostering Sibling Rivalry.:

When you compare, rather praise the other child to your child, your child may secretly start loathing his own sibling. This may lead him to behave aggressively, pick fights, tease and even hit each other. You are also passing across the message that the better performing child is more favored and loved. As a result, your children may start belittling himself

POSITIVE COMPARISON APPROACH TO HELP YOUR CHILD

Set benchmarks instead of comparisons:
Appreciate the effort, even if he secures 2 marks more than the previous exam. This builds the confidence.

Encourage to cope with the weakness:
Ask if your children need any help. Support him.

Praise their
Strengths: Whatever task your child performs well, appreciate it.

Do not Set Up Unrealistic Expectations:
If your girl wants to become a writer, do not force her to take up engineering. She may be smart, intelligent, but lacking aptitude and interest, which are detrimental for success in any field.

Provide unconditional support and love:
If your kid does not score well, do not make him feel that he has let you down or embarrassed you. Always support your child. Engage in a pep talk, encourage him to practice more and always appreciate his efforts in public.

Remember that every child is unique and that they have

different levels of interests, different strengths and weaknesses and quit comparisons.

PARENTAL AND PEER PRESSURE.

Save yourself and your kid from undue pressure for performance. It is more in the parents than children: - this trait of competing and comparing. Do not force your kid to pursue skating classes if he does not like to do so, he may be more interested in squash. Let him follow his interests and he is sure to excel therein with flying colors. Your self-esteem as parents should not be linked to your child's performance in school or sports. Remember, you are not your child; and realize it every time you push your child towards something that he does not want to do.

Now if your child complains that “you always take his side” or “you always support him, not me”, then do pay heed to his feelings. He is not voicing his feelings out of blue, maybe your actions – verbal or non-verbal make this evident to him? Be more careful about this.

Remember, neither you can nor your child can be a perfect mother or son encompassing excellence in all fields of academics, sports or relation-wise. Everyone has to face different challenges; the situation differs from home to home. If you will think deeply, your two children will differ in their sets of abilities and skills. Just be proud of your children for what they are. Give them your love and strive to build a confident person out of your child.

As Theodore Roosevelt aptly put: Comparison is the thief of joy

So do not rob your little one of the joy of childhood. Give him the space to grow!

- Know the value of boundaries

People talk a lot about the need for "boundaries," but what does this word really mean? As a parent, you can think of a boundary as the line you draw around yourself to define where you end and where your child begins. This is not always easy and we have to face it, kids push the boundaries every day, all the time. They are wired-up to test us and see how far they can go; as it is in their nature. As parents, we sometimes cross boundaries ourselves in our attempts to fix things for them. Understand that one of our most important jobs as parents is to stay loving and separate from our children. We do this by clearly defining our principles, staying in our role as parents, and sticking to our bottom lines.

- Setting their Eating Patterns for Life

By teaching your children healthy eating habits, and modeling these behaviors in yourself, you can help your children maintain a healthy weight and normal growth. Also, the eating habits your children pick up when they are young will help them maintain a healthy lifestyle when they are adults.

Your child's health care provider can evaluate your child's weight, height and explain their BMI and let you know if your child needs to lose or gain weight or if any dietary changes need to be made.

Some of the most important aspects of healthy eating are portion control and cutting down on how much fat and sugar your child eats or drinks. Simple ways to reduce fat intake in your child's diet and promote a healthy weight include serving:

*Low-fat or non-fat dairy products
*Poultry without skin
*Lean cuts of meats
*Whole grain breads and cereals
*Healthy snacks such as fruit and veggies
*Also, reduce the amount of sugar-sweetened drinks and salt in your child's diet.

- Communicate

Communication with children and babies is essential for their relationships and development.

Good communication involves listening and talking in ways that make children feel important and valued..

Communicating well with children helps them develop skills for communicating with others.

- Set clear targets

To better our chances of triumph, it is a good idea to start with a plan, and write it down. So here is a six (6) step plan for setting clear goals this year, following them should help keep your resolutions rolling along.

THE RULE OF PARENTING I

1. Be clear and specific with what you want to achieve. Do not just say you want to get fit or healthy, say you want to run a mile in 6 minutes, say you want to lose 10 pounds. Make it a clear goal that you can measure.

2. Break the goal down into steps. Have smaller goals to reach throughout the year, and reward yourself with something when you reach them.

3. Track your progress. We feel good about ourselves when we can see our improvements. There are many great applications out there with which you can do this, I recommend Lift.

4. Acknowledge your weaknesses, and take note of any setbacks. If you know when you are likely to trip up then you can prepare yourself in advance, or avoid it altogether.

5. Be accountable, and get a friend to make sure you follow through. When you do not go for your weekly run, or you indulge in that chocolate cake, set consequences–donations to a charity works well, try creating a commitment contract on Stick.

6. Make Sure you have Fun. If you are enjoying the ride down that long road to a new one you will likely fly past it, and be far less likely to give up.

What is better, with repeated success in achieving your goals, the plan you have in place and the method you use to reach them can form a habit. Each new challenge you succeed in will make the next one even easier. The thrill and rush of success never wears off, instead, with each accomplishment you will only increase your appetite for more new and exciting challenges.

- Do not be a Nag

The Negative Consequences of Nagging Children

1. It makes them feel incompetent.

2. It makes them feel manipulated.

3. It emphasizes the negative instead of the positive.

4. It alienates them.

4. It provides no long-term solution.

Each of these are fully described below.

1. It Makes Them Feel Incompetent

Parenting is a challenging job and, along the way, we pick up bad habits. One of these is nagging. In an effort to protect our children and prevent them from suffering the consequences of their behavior, mom and dads can begin to nit-pick, scold, complain, and kvetch.

As our youngsters grow into teenagers and start making their own choices, we feel a sense of the loss of control that causes us to turn it up a notch. The simple truth, though, is that nagging does not work. In fact, it can actually make our kids feel incompetent and, thus, become overly dependent on us.

When parents go on and on, kids tune them out. Researchers have shown that the human brain can keep only four 'chunks' of information or unique ideas in short-term (active) memory at once. These amounts to about 30 seconds or two sentences of speaking.

— Melanie Greenberg, psychologist and parenting expert

2. It Makes Them Feel Manipulated

Dr. Robert Myers, a clinical psychologist who has worked with children and adolescents for over 25 years, warns that nagging weakens the parent-child bond. Children simply tune it out because it is so unpleasant and “the more you nag, the less they hear,” he says. When carping Moms and Dads want to have a serious talk about drugs, sex, or other weighty issues, they should not be surprised when their children turn a deaf ear.

Dr. Myers explains that adolescents who get nagged feel manipulated and, therefore, resist it with all their might. Wanting to assert their independence and make their own decisions, teens become strong-willed and even defiant when parents pressurize them to do something. Instead of reacting to their insubordination by nagging even more, moms and dads should see their children response as normal and healthy. It simply means that they are growing up and separating from parental authority.

Catching our children doing something positive and complimenting them is far more effective than nagging.

3. It Emphasizes the Negative Instead of the Positive

Dr. Myers states that nagging harms the parent-child relationship because it is negative. He cautions that: “Nagging is a way of finding faults, and it tends to wear people down instead of build them up.” When moms and dads do it excessively, their children feel defeated. They figure that they cannot do anything right so they might as well stop trying.

A more effective strategy is to catch children doing something positive and praise their efforts. Parents can increase extrinsic motivation by offering age-appropriate rewards. They can, for example, award stickers, little toys, or a trip to the park/restaurant for younger children and extra television or computer time for older ones. Moreover, moms and dads should never underestimate the power of a simple compliment, especially with adolescents. Saying: "I appreciate how you filled the car with petrol/gas after borrowing it" means a lot more to teens than parents may imagine.

One thing we can do, when we become aware of our expertise in nagging and the reasons for it, is to appreciate the side benefits of not nagging. Parents who stop nagging and use substitute behavior always report reduced stress and positive consequences. Arguments drop significantly, and parents and teenagers learn to get along without the constant bickering.

5. It Alienates Them:

I found a book 'Stop Arguing with Your Kids' by Michael P.Nichols (Author and Family Therapist) extremely helpful as I parented my sons through the teen years. He advises moms and dads to be discerning when picking battles with their kids. He suggests letting go off the inconsequential (dirty socks on the floor, lights left on in the bathroom) to focus on the big-picture goal of rearing kids who will become responsible, independent adults with keen problem-solving skills.

Nichols says a common mistake moms and dads make is trying to control things that they do not need to control. He states, "When parents nit-pick their teenagers over little things, it just makes the children feel alienated. They may argue, they may say 'yes' to their parents, but whatever the outcome, they feel disrespected, they feel put down and they become antagonistic."

When it comes to nagging, parents should choose their battles carefully or they will antagonize their teens.

5. It Provides No Long-Term Solution

Parents nag for many reasons and are more likely to do so when feeling overwhelmed. While offering a quick fix in the moment, badgering our children does not stop the problem from recurring. Moreover, it usually comes at a high cost: damaging the parent-child relationship, making kids feel incompetent, and decreasing the likelihood of them becoming confident, capable adults.

A family counselor, says parents can achieve a long-term solution by establishing healthy boundaries between themselves and their youngsters. This, she claims, will greatly decrease or eliminate their impulse to nag. To accomplish this, she advises moms and dads to ask themselves an important question before opening their mouths: "What's my responsibility here, and what's my child's?" Pincus states: "When you move your focus off of your child and onto yourself by taking responsibility for how you act, your child will likely learn to be more accountable for his behavior."

The Reasons Parents Nag

Nagging is about us, not our children. It is a sign that our lives are out of sync and we need to make changes. The following are common reasons why we may be turning to this ineffective and destructive method of communicating with our youngsters:

We feel powerless in our lives: in our marriages, our jobs, and our families. Wanting to be in control of something, we target our children.

We feel anxious about the competitive world in which our children live. To cope with our fears, we push and nag our kids to get top marks, excel in athletics, have part-time jobs and internships, and be popular with the right crowd.

We are too busy and stressed out to help our children. When we are parenting on-the-fly rushing here and there and barking out orders—we forget that kids are little people who need our patience and guidance.

Our expectations are out-of-whack. Thinking that a kindergartner can clean their bedroom all by themselves or a teenager will always return the car with a full tank of gas is unreasonable and causes frustration.

We learned it from our parents. We nag because our moms and dads did so when we were growing up and now we are following their example because it is what we know.

The problem is, in our efforts to protect our children, we take valuable opportunities for learning away from them. Failure provides benefits that cannot be gained otherwise. Failure is a gift disguised as a bad experience. Failure is not the absence of success, but the experience of failure on the way to success.

Final Thoughts

The ultimate goal of parents is to rear children who will become independent, responsible adults. They accomplish this by allowing their children to make age-appropriate decisions for themselves and to learn from the consequences. If moms and dads accept that making mistakes is both essential and okay for youngsters, they will stop trying to control situations by nagging.

- Be consistent

How consistency improves children' behaviour

BEHAVIOUR

One of the simplest ways to improve a child's behaviour is to be more consistent.

Children love their parents to be consistent as they are able to predict how they will act. A consistent approach to discipline helps put kids in control of their behaviour.

Consistency implies that as parents we follow through and do as we say we will. It means that we resist giving kids second and third chances when they break the rules or behave poorly around others. When we let kids get away with two or three infractions of the rules, we often come down very hard eventually, which causes resentment. Acting early to prevent poor behaviour from escalating is the best approach.

Consistency also means both parents in a dual parent family get to act together and respond in similar ways when children are less than perfect. Children learn from a young age to play one parent off against the other when their standards differ or communication is poor. Sole parents need to be consistent with

how they react when children behave poorly.
A consistent approach is shown through a clear set of limits and boundaries that provide kids with structure and teaches them how to behave. Studies show that families with very few boundaries or rules are more likely to have children who behave poorly around others, or do not consider their own safety.

Children like limits and they also like to push against boundaries. One study has shown that kids will push parental boundaries about one third of the time. This is a normal, but irritating expression of a child's push for independence and autonomy. Some toddlers, teens and other tricky types will push twice that amount, which is very hard work indeed.

Consistency is often sacrificed by busy parents and put in the 'too-hard basket'. When parents are over-stretched, the last thing we want to do is engage in a battle with a strong-willed child over things that are sometimes petty issues. Besides, consistency can make a well-meaning parent who values relationships feel downright awful.

Giving in rather than holding your ground is not a smart long-term strategy. If you give in occasionally, kids will learn that if they push hard enough, or give that winning smile, you will eventually give in. Consistency is about being strong. It takes some backbone to be consistent.

THE RULE OF PARENTING I

- *Apologize if you get it wrong*

1. Own your feelings and take responsibility for them.

It is okay to be frustrated and it is okay to be upset sometimes – we tell our kids this all the time. Just remember that how we respond to those feelings is not always okay. It is not okay to yell or slam doors. Your kids are watching – so do not react in a way that you would not want them to emulate.

2. *Connect the feeling to the action.*

Explain in your apology why you felt the way you did. What happened that caused you to react that way? Do not use this as an opportunity to apportion blame ("I'm sorry I yelled, but I would not have hurt my foot if you had picked up your toys.")

3. *Apologize for the action.*

Point out which action of yours was inappropriate and explain why. Your kids will learn that they cannot act that way, either.

4. *Recognize your Child's Feelings.*

Show them that you understand they were hurt or scared. If your action was prompted by something your kids did or did not do, make sure they understand that your affection is not based on them meeting your expectations.

5. *Share how you Plan to Avoid this Situation in the Future.*

This is a great opportunity to teach your child how to learn from our mistakes and improve ourselves. Be specific in what you aim to do to keep from blaming others or yelling, for example.

6. *Ask for forgiveness.*
This can be as simple as "Could you forgive me?"

7. *Focus on making amends and solutions*
Offer to discuss and work out solutions to the issue with your child.

- Let them be better than you

It has always been the pride of the parents for their children to excel above them in terms of education, skill acquisitions and spiritually.

Be the role model your children deserve, good health, respectful, good behavior works much better.

- Different children need different rules.

Different rules: Just because your disciplinary strategy was successful with one child does not mean it will fly with your second (or third, or fourth). If a kid is not responding to your approach, make adjustments. He may just need a tighter leash than his sibling does. If incentives are not getting him to clean up his toys, you may have to take away his toys for a day. Figure out what works for each child, and go with it.

- Yelling is not the answer

Short answer: You are setting yourself up for a lifetime of shouting matches.

When children misbehave, yelling feels like a natural response, particularly if parents are burnt-out and their tolerance for nonsense abused. The messiness and monotony of parenting requires extreme patience, and yelling at your child is far easier and instinctive than pausing to react calmly. Yelling at your kids might feel like a release, or serve as a form of discipline. It may seem like yelling and screaming is the only way to get a kid's attention. It is important to understand the psychological effects of yelling at a child and why experts regard it as a less effective strategy.

As provocative as some behaviors may seem, little kids simply do not have the emotional sophistication to understand the frustration of an adult. Yelling at them would not suddenly trigger their understanding, but it might in fact have some adverse psychological effect. Some, long-term, with the potential to change the way their brains develop and process information. As hard as it may be to resist the temptation to scream, ultimately, yelling at kids is deeply unhelpful.

- Encourage them regardless.

Motivate children regardless of exam results,
parents must give their continuous supports to their children.

Results of public examinations are out. Students, parents, and even teachers become anxious around this time.

Despite reminding ourselves of the importance of learning, we still look at the grades scored.

Comparing the results of a child with another may bring more harm than good.

THE RULE OF PARENTING I

This may be viewed as a move towards getting the community to start viewing the performances of the students or children from a different perspective.

Acknowledge that every child or student has his own learning pace.

Hence, we should stop comparing our child's performance with that of other children as each child has different abilities, skills and talents.

They develop at a different pace. We should start nurturing ourselves to value the development of learning by looking at the students' learning process and the level of progress rather than merely counting the number of As scored in an examination.

As much as we want our children to do well in exams, we also need to remind ourselves and teach our children that there is always room for improvement whenever the results does not match their initial expectations.

Avoid putting too much pressure on children as it could lead them into depression.

Instead, we should lend a helping hand, inspire them to do better and give them the needed moral support to move on and see things positively.

Rewards and motivations should be inclusive. Not only those who excel should get rewards, the underperforming students should also be compensated and encouraged to try again.

Let us reflect on how we could play our role as parents, teachers and society during this daunting moment — one thing for sure, we need to always be ready to support our children whatever the outcome of their examination results.

2

2

THE RULES OF PARENTING II

Richard Templar " Some parents make it all look easy. They always seem to know the right things to do and say, however tricky the situation. They have a seemingly instinctive ability to raise happy, confident, well- balanced children.

Is there something they know that we do not know? Is it something that we could learn from them? The answer is a resounding yes. They know the Rules of Parenting

The Rules of Parenting are the golden principles and behaviors that will guide you smoothly through the challenges of raising children. They will help your children to handle themselves well, enjoy life, respect others, be decent and thoughtful, and to stand up for what they believe in. You will get more out of being a parent, and they will become all they can be.

The Rules of Parenting puts everything in perspective, you are in control and your children on the path to becoming successful, independent adults.

There is no job as important being a parent. How good could you be?

Teach Your Children
You must love God with all your heart, all your soul and all your strength. These words that I am commanding you today must be on your heart and you must inculcate them in your sons and speak of them you sit in your house and when you walk on the road and when you lie down and when you get up"

Children are the Heritage from the Lord, Psalm 127:3
Children are very special to God. They are mentioned 1,957 times in the Bible.

Child social development is the process by which an individual acquires the ability to behave in accordance with social expectation.

Child social behavioral patterns expected by society must be in consonance with socially approved patterns.
A father/mother is a leader in the home. Some qualities needed in a good leader are as follows: -

1. A good leader should set his/her heart to fulfill the task assigned to him. Acts 20:24; John 4:34; 2Tim.4:7. He must be a good finisher

2. He/ She must be an intercessor e.g. Moses (Ex.32:31-

32, Num.14:11-12, 15-20; (Era. 9:2-7)

3. He/ She must be able to motivate children and others to carry them along through his commitment. Joshua 24:15c-16; Neh.2:9-18; 1Tim. 4:12; Titus 2:7

4. He/ She must be a friend of Jesus Christ and learn from His Words to manifest greatness and good tidings like Esther and Abraham 2Chr.20:7

The Signs and Symptoms of Abnormal Behavior in Children

Children are cute when naughty. A few tantrums, arguments, and yelling occasionally is not abnormal. If such behavior becomes a daily occurrence, then it is a cause for concern. Here are some signs that indicate that your child's behavior is abnormal.

- Your child seems to have difficulty managing his emotions. He has frequent emotional outbursts and minor things bother him easily.

- It is not normal if your eight-year-old girl or boy becomes impulsive. They may display destructive behavior like hitting, throwing things, screaming, etc.

- Your otherwise talkative child withdraws into a shell, talks back and seems rude for no reason.

- Your little boy may be lying more often than you realize. Stealing or taking things that do not belong to them becomes a habit.

- Your child's behavior is affecting his performance at school. For example, your kid may be getting into fights, going late to class or missing classes.

- Spats and disagreements that your seven-year-old girl has with peers becoming a problem that affects her social life is not normal.

- The child's inability to focus on a thing per time and being restless

- The child's indulgence in sexual behavior that are not age appropriate.

- Your child starts questioning your instructions and does not respond to discipline. He may defy rules just to challenge you.

- It is not normal for children to harm themselves or even think about self-harm. Therefore, if they are harming themselves physically and having suicidal tendencies, you should be worried.

ACTIVITIES FOR CHILDREN WITH BEHAVIOR PROBLEMS

A highly effective way to deal with behavior problems in children, especially toddlers is through activities. Here are a few activities that are quite helpful which you may consider trying.

1. Prayer and Fasting (Matt. 9:37, Matt. 17:21, Matt. 21:22) Teaching children how to pray because prayer is very essential to a child's life so that He or She will not fall into the hands of evil doers.

2. Storytelling (Bible Stories) is yet another activity that engages their imagination and lets them use their energy in a positive way. This activity also helps you get an insight into their frame of mind.

3. Bible Game it is an exciting way to teach children the word of God and learn positive values.

Benefits of the Bible stories

- Provides a strong base for spiritual living
- Keeps children from sin
- Prepares them to witness or evangelize
- The scripture becomes part of them and directs them in decision- making.
- The Holy Spirit will remind them at an

appropriate time

- Knowing and memorization is easier at childhood.

4. Play good behavior games and read child behavior books that can teach the children good- deeds such as kindness, sharing, waiting and saying nice things to each other. When they learn that the good things can be rewarding, they would not try the bad ones.

5. Exercise or physical activities are perhaps the best means to let off the steam. When your child gets excited or angry, getting them to play outside can help relieve them of the energy. If a child's energy is not properly channeled, they tend to release it in the ways they know – tantrums, destructive behavior, acting out, etc.

6. Role-playing is an excellent activity that can teach your children to control impulses. One of the major factors affecting children behavior is the lack of self-control.

7. Ask your child to read aloud the Bible or his/ her writings. You can try this at bedtime when they are still full of energy and need an activity to calm down and relax.

Random misbehavior is the right of a child. Do not try to clamp down on it with your disciplinary ways. Let your children understand that you were once a child before you became a parent and you are in the best position to put them in the right social and Godly parenting way through Jesus Christ. However, if you see consistent and severe behavior problems in your child, then you need to take appropriate action. If you think that the situation is out of your hands, do not hesitate to approach a child behavior specialist, therapist or a counselor.

Remember, before you label your child as bad, try understanding the child's behavior to determine the root cause. With the right approach and professional help, behavioral issues in children can be fixed. After all, you want your child to grow into a loving, kind, intelligent and reasonable person, right?

Example of Misbehavior of Children in the Bible.

The Bible mentioned instances of misbehavior of children. A mob of children mocked God's prophet Elisha of ancient Israel. They taunted Elisha by saying, “Go up, you bald head.” As a result, they blasphemed God. Jehovah caused bears to claw forty-two of those juvenile delinquents.

2 Kings. 2:23, 24. They deserved severe treatment for calling Elijah a bald head, disrespect for the sacred was involved. The taunt “Go up, you bald head” called for vengeance by the Almighty God. It suggested that the prophet's presence was unwanted and for him to clear out of the territory. It is likely that adults were responsible for this misbehavior.

Children sometimes misbehave by reflecting the actions of adults, including their parents. The childish taunting was a manifestation of the attitude of adults around. It may have been prompted by adults who disliked the prophet. At any rate, the children were punished for their blasphemy. Proverbs 20:11 states: "Even a child is known by his actions, whether his behavior is pure and right."Youthfulness alone does not save children who speak irreverently of God, even if such wicked and irresponsible behavior were copied from their parents. Parents should help such children in changing their behavior, to respect elders always and to show utmost reverence for persons or things that are sacred, as a better example for children is an important discipline strategy.

3

3

BIBLICAL VALUES FOR MOULDING A CHILD IN THE WAY OF THE LORD

SELF-CONTROL

God teaches us how to live right. Titus 2:11-12 "God has shown us how kind he is by coming to save all people.

He taught us to give up our wicked ways and our worldly desires and to live decent and honest lives in this world.

THE HOLY SPIRIT, OUR COMFORTER, HELPS US TO BEHAVE

Galatian 5:22-23 "God's spirit makes vs. loving, happy, peaceful, patient, kind, good, faithful, gentle and self – controlled. There is no law against behaving in any of these ways.

We invite lots of problems into our lives if we can't control ourselves.

Proverb 25:28; "Losing Self-Control leaves you as helpless as a city without a well"

Sometimes it is hard to do right, but God promises to help us in those times. 1 Corinthians 10; 13; you are tempted but God can be trusted not to let you be tempted for much, and he will show you how to escape from your temptation.

SHOW LOVE TO EVERYONE

1. Show kindness to everyone (Ephesians 4:32)
2. Learn to forgive others (Luke 6:38)
3. Help others (Isaiah 41:6)
4. Don't steal (Exodus 20:15)
5. Don't cheat (Hebrews 13:18)
6. Don't lie (Proverb 12:7)
7. Obey your Parents (Eph.6:1)
8. Be careful in what you say and do (Luke 6:31)

God teaches us how to live right:

Titus 2:11-12:

"God has shown us how kind he is by coming to save all people. He taught us to give up our wicked ways and our worldly desires and to live decent and honest lives in this world."

The Holy Spirit, our Comforter, helps us to behave:
Galatians 5:22-23:

"God's Spirit makes us love, happy, peaceful, patient, kind, good, faithful, gentle, and self-controlled. There is no law against behaving in any of these ways."

We invite problems into our lives when we cannot control ourselves:

Proverbs 25:28:

> "Losing self-control leaves you as helpless as a city without a wall."

Sometimes it is hard to do right, but God promises to help us in those times:

1 Corinthians 10:13:

> "You are tempted in the same way that everyone else is tempted. But God can be trusted not to let you be tempted too much, and he will show you how to escape from your temptations."

OBEDIENCE

God does not want a PART of us to obey Him. He wants ALL of us to obey Him:

Leviticus 18:4:

> "I am the LORD your God, and you must obey my teachings."

It is never too late to turn away from the wrong things we do to obey God:

Nehemiah 1:9:

> "But you also said that no matter how far away we were,

we could turn to you and start obeying your laws. Then you would bring us back to the place where you have chosen to be worshiped."

Obedience brings many blessings, such as friendship with God:

John 14:23:

"Jesus replied: If anyone loves me, they will obey me. Then my Father will love them, and we will come to them and live in them."

WHOLESOME TALK

We need to use what we say to help others feel better, not hurt them:

Ephesians 4:29:

"Stop all your dirty talk. Say the right thing at the right time and help others by what you say."

Controlling what we say is hard, but if you work at it, it will be easier to behave in other areas too:

James 3:2:

"All of us do many wrong things. But if you can control your tongue, you are mature and able to control your whole body."

Don't start arguments, stop them!

Proverbs 15:1:

"A kind answer soothes angry feelings, but harsh words stir them up."

TREATMENT OF OTHERS

Put others first, before yourself, and you will please God:

Philippians 2:3:

"Don't be jealous or proud but be humble and consider others more important than yourselves."

God showed great kindness to us by sending Jesus. We need to show this same kindness to others:

Ephesians 4:31-32:

"Stop being bitter and angry and mad at others,don't yell at one another or curse each other or ever be rude. Instead, be kind and merciful, and forgive others, just as God forgave you because of Christ"

Here are what children would like their Sunday school teachers to follow.

1. *Thou shalt accept my youthfulness.*

I need tender direction and loving leadership. Constant criticism and raised eyebrows make me feel foolish and inadequate.

2. *Thou shalt accept my imperfections.*

Please do not expect perfection whenever you assign a task to me. I really do learn by my mistakes.

3. *Thou shalt accept my limitations.*
My hands are small and sometimes I seem awkward and clumsy. Please be patient with me.

4. *Thou shalt show me the way to go.*
When I show off, I am really asking for affirmation and reassurance. Could you please give me gentle guidance, so my behaviour does not become my attitude?

5. *Thou shalt welcome me.*
If I am new to your class, please take the time to explain the routine and show the other children that you are glad to see me (even if you thought your class was big enough already).

6. Thou shalt expect the best from me.
Please do not have preconceived ideas of me. I have the tendency to live up to your expectations. Expect me to behave appropriately.

7. *Thou shalt make the Word of God come alive for me.*
Find creative ways to teach me about the power of God, the ministry of Jesus, and all of God's Word.

8. Thou shalt help me know and do what is right.
Nobody needs to show me how to sin (it comes naturally), but somebody please care enough to lovingly discipline me when I act inappropriately.

9. *Honour my father and mother with good communication.*

Talking to my parents could help you discover my fears, my joys, my problems, my talents, my weaknesses, and my strengths.

10. *Thou shalt pray for me.*

You know, you may be the only person in the whole world who talks to God about me. I need you to ask God to help me.

TIME TO PRAY

1. Before you start a new day – ask Him to help you
2. Before meals – thank Him for the food
3. When you are afraid- ask for courage
4. When you are lonely or sad - ask Him to help you be happy
5. When you are in need – ask Him to forgive you
6. When you have sinned – ask Him to forgive you
7. When you are sick – ask Him for healing

SIX WAYS TO MANAGE MISBEHAVIOUR OF A CHILD

- Scolding, nagging and punishing does not work if the goal is to manage misbehavior without damaging your relationship with your child or the child's self-esteem.

-

There are better, more effective ways to deal with misbehaviors.

- Recognize the root of the problem.
- Recognize that misbehavior is a crude form of problem-solving
- The child's basic needs not being met.

- Listen to the child carefully and show love.

SIX LESSONS CHILDREN NEED TO LEARN
- CONTROLLED
- HUMBLE
- RESILIENT
- RESPONSIBLE
- MATURE
- HONEST

1. **The Benefits of Self-Control**

Self-control includes the ability to: -
- delay gratification
- restrain impulses
- complete unpleasant tasks
- put others before self

IMPORTANCE OF SELF-CONTROL

Children who have greater self-control can resist temptation, even when it promises short-term rewards. In contrast, children with less self-control may be more likely to:
- Be aggressive
- Suffer depression
- Smoke or abuse alcohol or drugs
- Make poor choices in what they eat

One study found that children with greater self-control were less likely, as adults, to have health issues, financial stress and problems with the law, was led by Prof. Angela Duckworth of the University of Pennsylvania to conclude; "There may be no such thing as too much self-control."

HOW TO TEACH SELF-CONTROL

Learn to say No and Mean it.

Matthew 5:37

"Let your word 'Yes' mean yes, your 'No' no."

Young children might test a parent's resolve by throwing a tantrum-perhaps even in public. If the parent gives in, the child learns that tantrums are an effective way to get a no changed to a yes.

Saying no to your child now will help him to say no to himself later on, in life when tempted to take drugs or to engage in other harmful practices.

Teach your child to prioritize

" Make sure of the more important things."

Philippians 1:10

Help him/ her to identify both good and bad

" Whatever a person is sowing, this he will also reap" Galatians 6:7

Be a good role model

" I set the pattern for you, that just as I did to you, you should also do" John 13:15

HOW TO BE HUMBLE

Humble people are respectful, they do not behave arrogantly, nor do they expect preferential treatment from others.

Sometimes humility is regarded as weakness. In reality, it helps people recognize their faults and acknowledge their limitations.

IMPORTANT OF HUMILITY

Humility benefits relationships.

Humble people are more connected to others says the book "The Narcissism Epidemic", it adds that such people find it easier to relate to others and the wider world."

Humility benefits your child's future.

Learning to be humble will help your child positively now and in the future.

HOW TO TEACH HUMILITY

"If anyone thinks he is something when he is nothing, he is deceiving himself" Galatians 6:3

A child who learns to perform humble tasks at home is more likely to work well with others as an adult.

Encourage your child to apologize quickly.

Help your child to see where he is wrong and to acknowledge it.

Praise specific actions.

Simply telling a child that he or she is "awesome" does not encourage humility. Be specific.

HOW TO BE RESILIENT

A resilient person bounces back from obstacles and disappointments and this skill is acquired through experience. Just as a child cannot learn how to walk without occasional falls, he cannot learn how to succeed in life without experiencing occasional setbacks.

IMPORTANT OF RESILIENCE

Some children get discouraged when they meet with failure, adversity or criticism. Others give up entirely. However, they need to understand the following facts:

- Failure is inevitable in some endeavors. James 3:2
- Adversity affects everyone at some point. Ecclesiastes 9:11
- Correction is vital for learning. Proverbs 9:9

Resilience will help your child face life's challenges with confidence.

HOW TO TEACH RESILIENCE

When a child fails.

" The righteous one may fall seven times and he will get up again" Proverbs 24:16

A child who is able to bounce back from disappointments and mistakes is more likely to persevere when acquiring skills thereby becoming proficient at them.

Also, avoid fixing the problem for your child. Instead, help him create his own plan. You might ask him. 'What can you do to improve your understanding of the subject that is being taught?'

Constructive criticism

How can you help your child benefit from constructive criticism? When your child receives it-whether at school or anywhere else-resist the urge to say that the correction is unfair, instead, you could ask:

- Why do you think the correction was made?"
- What would you do to improve yourself?"
- What will you do, when next you are in this type of situation?"

Remember, constructive criticism will serve your child well both now and in the future (adulthood).

HOW TO BE RESPONSIBLE

Responsible people are reliable. A child's capacity to cooperate begins at fifteen months and his desire to willingly start pitching-in begins at around eighteen months" says the book "Parenting Without Borders". "In many cultures parents begin to hone their children's helpfulness especially between the ages of five and seven, and children of this age range competently assist in many domestic tasks."

IMPORTANT OF BEING RESPONSIBLE

The term "boomerang generation" describe young adults... Training your Child for Adulthood.

HOW TO TEACH RESPONSIBILITY

"There are benefits in every kind of hard work" Proverbs 14:23
Children who are taught to be responsible will be able to manage their lives more effectively as adults.
"Listen to counsel and accept discipline, in order to become wise in your future" Proverbs 19:20
Children make mistakes and when they do, it is vital that parents should own up to their mistakes and failures which will in turn instruct your children

- To be honest and admit their errors
- To avoid blaming others
- To avoid making excuses
- To apologize, when appropriate

MATURE/ADULT GUIDANCE

Children need adults (such as their parents) in their lives who can provide leadership and advice.

IMPORTANT OF ADULT GUIDANCE

- Children spend much of their days in school, where students outnumber teachers and other adults.
- After school, some youths return to a home that is empty because both parents have to work
- One study found out that children between 8 and 12 years of age spend an average of about six hours on entertainment, media each day.

HOW TO PROVIDE GUIDANCE

- Spend time with your children

A child who looks to adults for guidance is more likely to display wisdom and maturity later on in life. Parents remain the major source of influence on their child's attitude and behavior through adolescence and into young adulthood as they spend time with their children to share your views, values and experiences with them.

MORAL VALUES.(HONESTY)

People with moral values have a clear sense of right and wrong.

IMPORTANCE OF MORAL VALUES

Children are inundated with distorted messages on morals, whether from their schoolmates/ classmates, the music they listen to, or the movies and TV shows they watch. Such influences can challenge their beliefs concerning what is right and what is wrong.0

HOW TO TEACH MORAL VALUES

"Mature people... have their powers of discernment trained to distinguish both right and wrong." Hebrews 5:14

Children who see their parents display honesty are most likely to resist temptations to be dishonest when alone.

REINFORCE MORAL VALUES

"Maintain a good conscience" 1 Peter 3:6

- Commend good behavior. If your child displays good

moral values in what he does, praise him for it and explain with examples and when he confesses his wrong doing, commend him for his honesty

- Correct bad behavior. Help your children accept responsibility for their actions. Children should be made to be aware of their wrongs.

THE REASON CHILDREN MISBEHAVE

The reason children misbehave, 'you and I are adults'; we talk like adults, use deductive reasoning, think about the consequences of our actions and make informed decisions based on facts largely. Adults are not always wonderfully smart, though, we can and often do, fall prey to the "Little adult syndrome" when dealing with children. especially when they are misbehaving Christian parents who saturate their children's day with the love of God will naturally want to incorporate His standards during times of training and discipline. However, let us remember that God's word should be used to heal, not punish. It is a Band-Aid, not a weapon.

The collection of verses below can be used with your children when their hearts are soft after a misbehavior, you can also incorporate these truths during everyday conversation, while reading stories together or during family devotion times.

These verses are good complement to our Heart of the Spiritual Parenting.

Obedience

God does not want a Part of us to obey Him. He wants All of us to obey Him;

Leviticus 18:4 I am the Lord your God and you must obey my teachings.

It is never too late to turn away from wrong doings to obeying God;

Nehemiah 1;9

"But you also said that no matter how far away we were, we could turn to you and start obeying your laws. Then you would bring us back to the place where you have chosen to be worshipped.

Obedience brings many blessings, such as friendship with God.

John 14:23

"Jesus replied if anyone loves me, they will obey me. Then my father will love them and we will come to them and live in them.

Wholesome Talk

We need to use what we say to help others feel better, not hurt people, Ephesians 4:29, "Stop all your dirty talk, say the right thing at the right time and help others by what you say.

CONTROLLING WHAT WE SAY IS HARD, but if you

work at it, it will be easier to behave in other areas too. James 3:2 " All of us do many wrong things. But if you can control your tongue, you are mature and able to control your whole body.

Don't Start Arguments

Stop them. Proverb 15:1. A kind answer soothes angry feelings but harsh words stir them up.

Treatment of others: Put others first, before yourself pleases God: Philippians 2:3 "don't be jealous or proud, but be humble and consider others more important than yourselves"

God Showed Great Kindness.

God showed great kindness to us by sending Jesus, we need to show this same kindness to others: Ephesians 4:31-32, "Stop being bitter, angry and mad at others. Do not yell at one another or curse each other, or ever be rude. Instead, be kind and merciful and forgive other, just as God forgave you because of Christ.

2 Timothy 2:15

"Study to shew thyself approved unto God, a workman that needeth not to be ashamed, rightly dividing the word of truth."

Spirituality is an inner sense of relationship to a higher power that is loving and guiding who is God. The important point is that spirituality encompasses our relationship and dialogue with this higher presence.

And the lord God formed man of the dust of the ground and breathed into his nostrils the breath of life and Man became a living soul Genesis 2:7

One of the greatest weapons of the enemy against parenting in these last days is IGNORANCE; Parents must be informed concerning the things of the Spirit. 1 Corinthians 12:1

Spiritual parenting is a call for parents to be intelligent, informed and skillful concerning the things of the spirit.

Parents cannot continue to invest in confusion in this century where raising Godly children is becoming more challenging. Raising a Godly Child will become easier by training and by help of the Holy Spirit for parents who are wise in the spirit.

We need to understand that parenting is not to be carried out by human strength but by the strength of the LORD.

Parenting is spiritual; we understand through the Bible that Man is a living soul, while Biology defines man as a living thing. This implies that when two things come together to conceive they give birth to a thing. What we should understand is that marriage is not a thing, but spiritual union from God and that sex is more of a spiritual exchange created by God, that must not be viewed only as a physical thing (act).

BIBLICAL VALUES FOR MOULDING A CHILD IN THE WAY OF THE LORD

Spiritual parenting demands that parents should be filled with the knowledge of God. In every Child, there is a king, which means Knowledge in God!

How do you raise your child to become a King that will reign in his/her generation without the knowledge of God?

The major deficit in spiritual parenting is LACK- Low Attitude Concerning the Knowledge of God!

The attitude of many parents towards the knowledge of God is poor and they are not bothered about it, and satan rejoice in keeping them in ignorance.

The Bible declares that weeping shall continue until the Books are opened.

Spiritual Parenting requires teaching our children divine truth from the Book of the truth, The Bible.

In homes where the Bible is the instruction manual, it will not suffer from mass production of misbehaviours in children and adults that society is producing these days.

The first Assignment for Spiritual Parenting is to store up the knowledge and wisdom of God for our children. We must make sure we have Spiritual Milk and meat in abundance to feed them with .

BIBLICAL VALUES FOR MOULDING A CHILD IN THE WAY OF THE LORD

Let the word of God dwell richly in you, so that you can have something to dish out to your children.

Fire up your Spiritual Knowledge: You need to cultivate the spiritual soil for them (your children) to grow into spiritual giants that God has designed them to be. Therefore awake from slothfulness to attend appropriately to the children with greatness whom the Lord has given you

Rise up to your responsibility, your child cannot live by bread alone, you are both a bread winner and a soul winner. Win the souls of your children for Christ. Soul winning begins at home. As you 'chase' bread, you must make time out to chase God and raise a Godly Generation.

4

4

SPIRITUAL ASSIGNMENT IN PARENTING

Like arrows in the hand of a warrior, so are children born in one's youth. - Psalm 127:4

Karunamayu says *"Many of you may find your children very different from the previous generations. We always hear people saying that their 2 year or 3 year old knows how to use the mobile phones, can operate an iPad or turn on the TV, or that they are much smarter in something else in comparison to what they were at that age. They feel great pride in saying it".*

Children today are children of the New Age. They have come here on Earth, many from different dimensions, to help Earth in this great period of evolution. In the spiritual language, this evolution is called Ascension or the rise in consciousness.

These children are the bringers of the new energies, the energies that have their base in Love.

SPIRITUAL ASSIGNMENT IN PARENTING

Our generation and the previous generations have fed on the energy of fear. Parents have very commonly used fear strategies to get their children to eat, do their homework, sleep on time and basically toe the line.

Remember hearing 'Eat now or I will call the police! Don't go there!, There is a monster there and so on? Parents, grandparents, great grandparents have all lived on the energies of fear and its accompanying emotions of anger, jealousy and hatred. Do you remember racial discriminations, discriminations based on religion and tribes? Or jealous feelings when one sees a friend buying a new expensive car or house? Or anger, which does not even require examples.

The new age children have come to help earth rise above these harmful and detrimental emotions so that Earth can evolve into the higher dimension which is based on Love and Joy.

> "And she shall bring forth a son, and thou shalt call his name Jesus: For he shall save his people from their sins." Matthew 1:21

There is a calling before conception. There is something each child is fashioned to become before been formed in the womb. Before I formed thee and before thou came forth out of the womb I sanctified thee and I ordained thee a prophet unto the nations.

SPIRITUAL ASSIGNMENT IN PARENTING

Jeremiah 1:5

"Every child is separated from the womb for a specific assignment"

But when it pleased God, who separated me from my mother's womb and called me by his grace to reveal his son in me, that I might preach him among the heathen; immediately I conferred not with flesh and blood;

Galatians 15:16

Listen, o isles, unto me and hearken ye people from far, the Lord have called me from the womb from the bowels of my mother hath he made mention of my Name…

And now saith the Lord that formed me from the womb to be his servant to bring Jacob again to him. Isaiah 49:1 5a

YES, YOUR CHILD HAS A CALLING

a. Calling- High places to occupy in life
b. High calling- Important Assignment to fulfill
c. Important calling- Life to impact
d. Life calling- Destiny to fulfill

From the above scripture, I strongly believed that the second assignment of Spiritual Parenting is to desire to know your children Spiritual callings and start praying right from the time the child is conceives in the womb.

It is important to know that desire precede praying; therefore, I say unto you, what things so ever ye desire, when ye pray and believe that ye receive them and ye shall have them. Mark 11:24

How many parents desire to know what God has set aside for our children from the womb and while they are babies?

Desire – Pray – Believe – Receive – Have

Often times, the major prayer point of pregnant women is for safe delivery of their children which is good and wonderful. The Bible says our women shall deliver like the Hebrew women notwithstanding the core prayer should be more on the physical delivery as well as the spiritual delivery of the baby's calling.

Women should understand that they are rich in blessing and also blessing to the world.

The mother of our Lord Jesus Christ carried one blessing in her womb for nine months and these blessings brought billions of souls into eternal blessings.

You can help your child to discover his or her calling or assignment, parent therefore no limit to whatever you desire to know. There is no Godly desire that doesn't attract divine manifestation.

But ye have unction from the Holy Spirit and ye know all things 1 John 2:20

SPIRITUAL ASSIGNMENT IN PARENTING

And this confidence that we have, that if we ask anything according to his will, he heareth us. It is God's will that we should desire and know the specific assignment that God called our children for;

God can reveal our child assignment to us through

2. Dream Matthew 1:20-21
3. Prophesy Luke 1:67 – 80
4. Revelation Luke 2:26 – 32
5. Holy Spirit Psalm 51 - 11

What is God saying about your children? Do we have interest in knowing our children more?

Yes, today many are not privileged to have angelic visitation like that of old but we have the word of truth the Word of God and Holy Spirit that tells on the mind of God to reveal to us whatsoever we desire to know.

I pray that our eyes of understanding be open to desire to know what God's calling for our children is: The Bible say, whatever ye desire when you pray.

Desire matters! If we desire it, we can pray for it, we can have the knowledge of what God design our children for our children are here on planet earth to meet a specific need, they are here on purpose for purpose and to be a wonder to many.

Parent, let fire up our desire to know the area of greatness where God is calling our children to let begin to pray for them right when there are in the womb.

IN SUMMARY

- Every child has a calling
- Every parent can desire to know their calling even when there are in the womb
- God will for parent is to know the calling of their children
- Parent assignment is praying for understanding spiritually of what their children assignment on earth is

Signs and Wonder! (SAW)

The Bible say, the children that God has given to us are for signs and wonder.

The word further says- Our seed shall be great in the land, And so many other promises about our children. But these are promises waiting for us to activate them in the place of prayer:

Spiritual Assignment of Parent Is Prayer

PRAY TO SEE! The word seeds refer to our Children, for our seeds to be great, we need to pray to see the greatness, hold that picture in our heart and always pray to see what our seed will become, the GAP between Human being and human becoming is close when one Go And Pray!

Pray to God to open our eyes concern the bundle of blessing we carry in our womb, what is in our womb- is wonder of multiple blessings. It is more than bone and flesh, that is the reason we need not to consult our reasoning about them but consult God Almighty who sew the together in the womb, consult God to know their calling, consult God to discover what their assignment are: -ASSIGNMENT

For your child to be a sign and wonder to many in his generation. You have a responsibility to pray. Pray to see the sign, pray to see the wonder, pray to see the potential, pray for the manifestation of what God has put in him/her.

Genesis 49:25

Even by the God of thy father, who shall help thee and by the Almighty who shall bless thee with blessings of heaven above, blessings of the deep that lieth under, blessings of the breasts and of the womb.

Psalm 127:3

Lo, children are a heritage of the Lord, and the fruit of the womb is his reward.

Are you ready to pray?

There are prayers points to pray for discovering your children calling and assignment.

- You the destiny of my baby/children, arise by fire and move into signs and wonder in the Name of Jesus.
- Every power at the gate of death, killing good things in the lives of my baby/children die in the Name of Jesus.
- Every cloud of darkness covering the open heavens of my baby/children, clear away by fire, in the Name of Jesus.
- I set the blood of Jesus between satan and the open

heavens of my children and I command them to enter into new era of progress in the Name of Jesus.

- I revoke every satanic decree upon the life of my baby with the Blood of Jesus, in the Name of Jesus.
- I raise the staff of prayer to divide the Red Sea standing between my firstborn and his miracle of supernatural
- O Lord open my eye to the destiny of my Baby in the womb in Jesus Name
- Every agent of disgrace, backwardness, shame and reproach delegated against my Baby, ground open and swallow them, in Jesus Name
- You my baby in the womb hear the Word of the Lord and Manifest positively in Jesus Name
- You my baby/children, I prophecy into your lives, receive divine visitation and enjoy covenant of peace in the Name of Jesus.
- Every negative words or curse on my baby/children back to sender in Jesus Name.
- Every arrow of affliction, fashioned against the destiny of my children backfire in the Name of Jesus
- Any power using my children's life to renew his life, I sentence you to sudden and untimely death, die in the Name of Jesus.
- Anointing of God over shadow my baby/children in the Name of Jesus.

5

5

MORE SPIRITUAL CONTENT

Train up a child in the way he should go: and when he is old, he will not depart from it.
-Prov. 22:6

Most Christian parents would probably agree that the spiritual training of their children is important, but they don't feel as if they have the time, energy, or qualifications to provide it. Many let this aspect of child-rearing fall by the wayside out of mere ignorance or fear of failure. You are wise to begin thinking about this part of your responsibility as parents as early as possible.

Spiritual training involves more than just sending your children to Church. It's basically a matter of living the principles you believe – letting Biblical truths permeate your conversation and using everyday incidents to make a point or illustrate a truth from God's Word. In other words, parental modelling is the most important piece of the puzzle. Kids need to see active faith demonstrated in their parents' lives. No one expects you to be perfect but your actions truly speak louder than your words. Letting your children see you read the Bible, for instance, shows them the relevance of Scripture to your life. It can also lead to some important discussions of spiritual things. Regular prayer times are also important. As your children grow, make the effort to pray with them about their personal struggles. When God answer a prayer, call it to your child's attention and thank the Lord for what He has done.

But of the tree of the knowledge of good and evil; thou shall not eat of it, for in the day that thou eatest thereof, thou shall surely die.

Gen 2:17

Every child that is born out of a woman is physically alive but Spiritually dead. The word " dead" in this context means the spirit is not active, dormant has no capacity to respond not yet activated, can't function or do anything.

Every child inherits the adamic nature of sin and this is core reason for the misbehavior in children. John 3:6

You will notice that some babies bite their mother breast to get attention.

Wickedness, anger, lies etc naturally flow in them because by one man (Adam) these ungodly natures enter into human race.

MORE SPIRITUAL CONTENT

The Godly content in Adam was replaced when Adam eats the fruit that God command them not to eat and resulted that the spiritual content in Adam was replace with a sin content.

SIN CONTENT VERSUS SPIRITUAL CONTENT

Through food, Adam was defeated. He lost the Godly nature in him and gain the nature of sin.

Sin separate man from the nature of God.
SIN means Separate It Now! Man was separated from the Spiritual nature and sin nature take over him.

> *For all have sinned and come short of the glory of God.*
> Roman 3:23

By one-man sin enter into the world and also by one-man righteousness enter into the whole world.

There is no need to debate this: Every one born of a woman is a Sinner-Children, boy, girl, teenager, adult – all have sinned! But the good news is that when we come to Christ, we receive the Godly nature back, get connect to our spirit and our spirit begins to grow into Christ like Spirit- we become a new creature and have dominion over sin. No longer a slave to sin.

Every child need to experience two birth

A. Born of woman
B. Born of God

MORE SPIRITUAL CONTENT

Spiritual Parenting is crucial at this point after our child is born out of a woman, it is our responsibility to help and guide our child to experience the most important birth that carry eternal benefits- Born of God

> *Man that is born of a woman is of few days and full of trouble.* -Job 14:1

No parent wants his/her child to experience few days and day full of trouble on earth.

> Our children can live long and enjoy a life of God on earth. Whoever is born of God has victory and can live Godly Spiritual life.
>
> Our child must be born again, the fruit of the righteous is a tree of life.
>
> Our children, the fruit of the womb is the fruit of the righteous, righteous children must be spiritual wise and train to choose the tree of life.

In the beginning, the tree of life and the tree of knowledge of good and evil occupy the Centre of the garden.

So also today, the tree of life and the trees of death is every present and occupy the decision Centre of our life. Take them to make diligently spiritual parenting called for guiding our children to choose life – by deliberately and intentionally train

them with spiritual content from the Bible.
My dear parents, can God say that for I know him, that he will command his children and his household after him and they shall keep the way of the Lord. Genesis 18:19

Joshua, says as for me and my house we shall serve the Lord. This day life and death is present to us but the Bible encourage us to choose life.

Parent decision to guide their physically alive but spiritual dead children in the path of life, the way of God will help their child to reach for the tree of life- Jesus Christ and by chosen tree of life, their spirit come alive and they become the child of God.

Parenting the children from children of men to the children of God is our responsibility and the Bible speaks about deep calleth unto deep at the noise of thy waterspouts: all waves and thy billows are gone over me. Psalm 42:7

The parent that are not deep in the things of God may not be able to reach to the deep spiritual deposit within the soul of their children talk less of calling it out.

Spiritual parenting one major assignment is called out the spiritual content that is dormant in their children.
But many parent and even children department are not helping in this area.

In fact, some church children department is not active, what they do on Sunday, Sunday is to give their biscuit and drink-feeding them physically.

Joshua encourages us to eat the WORD OF GOD, let your child eat the word of God every day. serve him/her with hot meals of spiritual bread, Today, we have daily bread for children, Godly children video, books and games that we can use to intentionally train our children in the way of the Lord. The rate of misbehavior in children is increasing daily because of what we feed them with.

Stop feeding them with Television content that are ungodly- the TV is of two content: -

A. Teach vision
B. Teach violence/virus

Spiritual parenting must take charge and deliberately help their children to watch TV programs that teaches vision to their children.

It has been research unto and discover that children that are violent in their action learn most from the violent video and game on Television and also from domestic violence from their parent.

Today, we have more Sinful content been display on our cable TV channels (some children enter evil net to watch dirty video that is designed to pollute the children's mind)
we shouldn't be deceived, deceivers are busy producing

gadgets and tools to program our young minds with evil we need wisdom to carefully select what we expose our children to.

We can't but feed them with spiritual milk and meat if we want the children to grow spiritual, wise and mature spiritually.

6

6

MORE SPIRITUAL CONNECTION

Then spake the woman who's the living child was unto the King, for her bowels yearned upon her son and she said, O my Lord, give her the Living child and in no wise slay it. But the other said, let it be neither mine nor thine, but divide it.

-1king 3:26

The worldly system is very desperate to take our living child and replace it with dead child. The weapon fashion against our living child is so subtle and cunning and spiritual parenting demand that we do more than correcting but more of connecting them to God.

The common traditional role of parenting by correcting them is good but let reach for the best strategies by connecting them to God and raise spiritual standard against the enemy over our children.

MORE SPIRITUAL CONNECTION

Let examine three stronghold connection that want our child dead spiritually

1. Internet connection
2. Media connection
3. Street connection

These connections are target to exchange the lives of our children if you don't manage or train our children in the way of the Lord.

The street connection is design with a slogan if you can't join them, you cannot beat them, you cannot be part of them and you can't be considered as someone doing great things. But the silent motives of street connection are to initiate many into what is contrary to spiritual value and influence them with street value that it seems positive but the end thereof is death.

> *I am a companion of all-them that fear thee and of them that keep thy precepts.* -Psalms 119:63

The street connection is raising company of young one that operates on evil opinion instead of God's opinion. Satan is selling his opinion through street connection and he understand that opinion matters in dominion!
\
Yes, man is giving DOMINION freely but with a condition that he should submit himself to God; that is obedience to God.

Men that disobey God cannot have dominion! If they obey not, they shall perish by the Sword and shall die without knowledge.

> However, if they obey and serve Him they shall spend their days in prosperity and their years in pleasure.
> -Job 36:12,111

Spiritual parenting understanding is that there is a Sword in the street that is design to kill, steal and destroy our children but we also have the Sword of the Spirit that can protect, positioning and prosper our children.

The promise of street connection is prosperity and pleasure, which the world cannot give, the real prosperity and pleasure comes from God.

Psalm 118:25 let us know that God is the one sending prosperity and Psalm said at His right hand are pleasure forever more

Spiritual parenting must be wise that Sword in the street is strategically design to divide our children from the plan of God for their life.

INTERNET CONNECTION

The earth planet operating on a planet of instruction, there is no debate on the issue that everything on earth function by instruction. Even the scientist understands that there are set of coded instruction that earth operate with and through the Bible we have and hold the truth that earth comes into existence through the word of God. John1:1-3

That instruction the earth operate with is the word of God.

Genesis 1:9 And God said "let the waters under the heaven be gathered together unto one place, and let the dry land and it was so. Moreover, God called the dry land.

Earth appears at the command of God, God spoke and the earth comes into existence.

It is God's planet and God has a plan for his children. Jeremiah 29:11 the plan I have for you is plan of peace.

The internet is another planet on its own, check the content on the internet 80% of the content if not more is Satanic content designed to sell "Lust" to our children. Lust is living under sinful thoughts or living under satanic thought.

The core purpose is to steal the thought of God away from the heart of our children and replace it with his own SIM – (Sinful Instructional Manual).

Spiritual parenting calls for diligently guiding the hearts of our children in the area of content they allow in to their heart.

Heart is the Centre of all life issues, the heart of our children is the greatest resource of our future and we must protect it against the thieves that come through internet.

MORE SPIRITUAL CONNECTION

Internet is "enter net" or into-net, many act of misbehavior are learnt through the internet, the rate of disobedience, multiplication of violence and virus operate via this medium and Spiritual parenting has a weapon to destiny, every evil that internet wants to exchange the living child with dead child. The Devil has nothing to offer but suffering and death.

Let your child surf the net for more spiritual content that can help his/her growth spiritually.

Educate him/her on how to use internet to his advantage mentally and spiritually.

THE MEDIA CONNECTION

The media sound like "ME DIE"- Yes, many are dying spiritually daily because of various media gadgets. They call it the Social Media, yes, there are spiritual contents but the devil has a load of sinful content on the social media.

The book 'Hold On to Your Kids' says: "Young people are turning for instruction, modeling and guidance not to mothers, fathers, teachers and other responsible adults but to... *their own peers"*

The class of social media keep taking attention every day, the social media like Facebook, Instagram and twitter doesn't give time for the children and adult to face the Book-Bible. Bible in no doubt is the best book that you can face in other to see who you are and see the picture of your future, see your dream, see your talent see your potential, see your career.

Whatsoever thing you desire to see is in the Bible- it is a spiritual mirror to see yourself clearly.

The Instagram, twitter, YouTube, Facebook, WeChat and others are loaded with content that can build and destroy.

Spiritual Parenting must not be ignorant of satanic devices that is formulate to frustrate the things of God in the life of our children.

Devil equally understand that every great vision start with a division. He sets out to divide our children and take them away (far) from the vision of God for their life.

One of my children said devil is foolish and God is wise. Yes, God is All wise, let me be bold to tell you; spiritual parenting is to make devil foolish and make our seed wise in handling and destroying devil devices.

Our seed shall be the head and not the tail, they shall be above only and not beneath in Jesus Name.

Our weapon is mightier through God to pull all the stronghold down and bring every thought (on social connection, internet, media connection) that is contrary to the thought of God into captivity.

MORE SPIRITUAL CONNECTION

Negative thought is a tool to bring people into captivity, *Spiritual Parenting* is the complete way of training the child in the way of the Lord, let your child be full of the thought of God, as a man thinketh inside so he is.

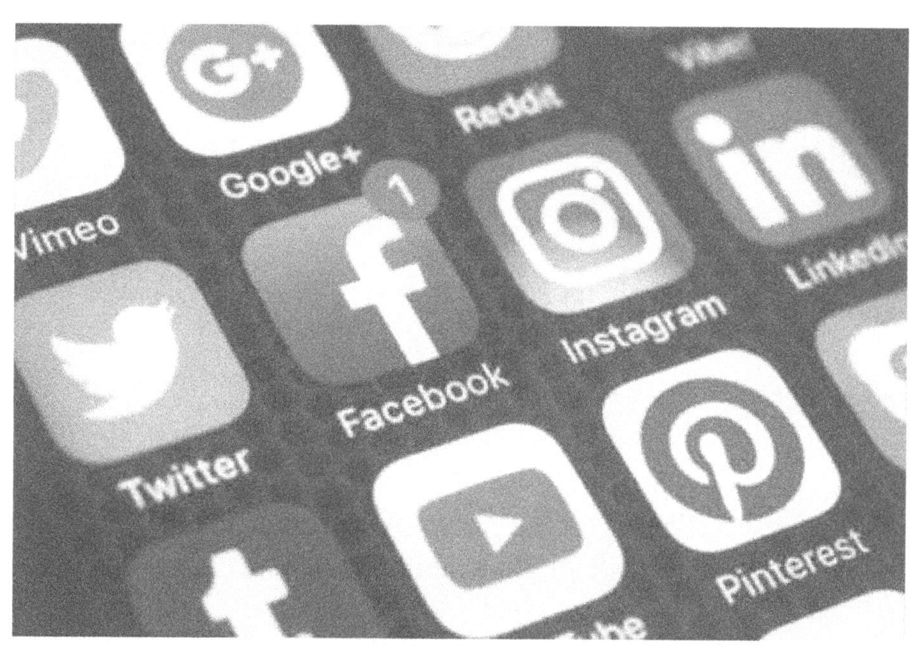
Vimeo
Google+
Reddit
1
Facebook
Instagram
Twitter
Pinterest

7

7

BAD SOCIAL CIRCLE

Who leave the paths of uprightness, to walk in the ways of darkness?
-Proverb 2:13

Does your social circle affect your habit building?
Your social life can play a major role in your digital life. Life is most rewarding when you are part of a group that supports each other through all the highs and lows life has to offer. Inspiring and being inspired by loved ones will allow you to discover your best self.

We live in a world of Facebook, Instagram, Twitter and LinkedIn, where everybody is aiming to "network" we are all aware of the benefits of knowing the right people in the right places. And having the right SOCIAL CIRCLE is the most effective way to meet individuals who can mold and enhance your thought process.

BAD SOCIAL CIRCLE

Choosing the right social circle means surrounding by nature. Many people in your life will eventually come across someone who is an expert in meditation. Only a few will remember that you are interested in that subject and try to help you out. They are the ones who need to be in your social circle.

There are two basic optionsfor our children.

Option 1 – Walk with Word
Option 2 – Walk with World

Spiritual parenting plays a vital role in teaching and directing the children to walk with God – walk in the path of Grace.

The increasing rate of disgrace, shame and disappointing many children bring to their parent today because of the path the parent ignorantly or unconsciously allow them to walk into.

Multitude of parent are FAR from getting the result they desire, and or FAR from harvest of rest and peace of mind from their children because they fail to teach their children to go for F.A.R (Follow After Righteousness).

> *The way of the wicked is an abomination unto the Lord, but He loveth him that followeth after righteousness.*
> -Proverb 15:19

The 21st century parenting is becoming more challenging because there are multitudes of path calling on our children to follow them. The common sentence today is following me/us on twitter, Instagram, Facebook.

Spiritual parenting has a responsibility to define who and what their children follow on social media. God, our ultimate spiritual parents give us the list of thing to follow in His Word.
Flee also from youthful lusts: but follow

- Righteousness
- Faith
- Charity
- Peace

With them that call on the Lord out of a pure heart.

Spiritual parenting must be spiritually smart to ensure that their children make friend on social media with them that call on the Lord out of a pure heart.

We should not be deceived by technology; it is a weapon both good and bad. It is the duty of spiritual parenting to use technology to his/her children advantage.

Technology can bring positive transformation to our children life and as well serve as "Transportation" to convey them from Godly character into ungodly character.

Our children must flee from any social media that represent "LUST " living under sinful thought "we must protect our child from social content that supply sinful contents to their productive mind.

BAD SOCIAL CIRCLE

Any circle of friendship that can pollute the children's mind and re-direct it toward ungodly activities should be total discouraged.

Spiritual parent understands the power of imitation. It is our duty to show and teach them how to imitate God. Otherwise they will imitate other, not only that, they will also imitate street personality that keep shouting "follow us" every second.

The peer pressure, social media and the program your children listen to determine what flow to their mind and reflex in their lives. The misbehavior of children will fail if we as parents fails to guide them to the Lord, The Bible says Teach up a Child the way His/her should, so that they will not depart from the Lord.

FOLLOW UP WHAT/WHO THEY ARE FOLLOWING

Children need proper direction or instruction, it is the job of the spiritual parenting to guide them and encourage them to follow the direction of destiny for their life.

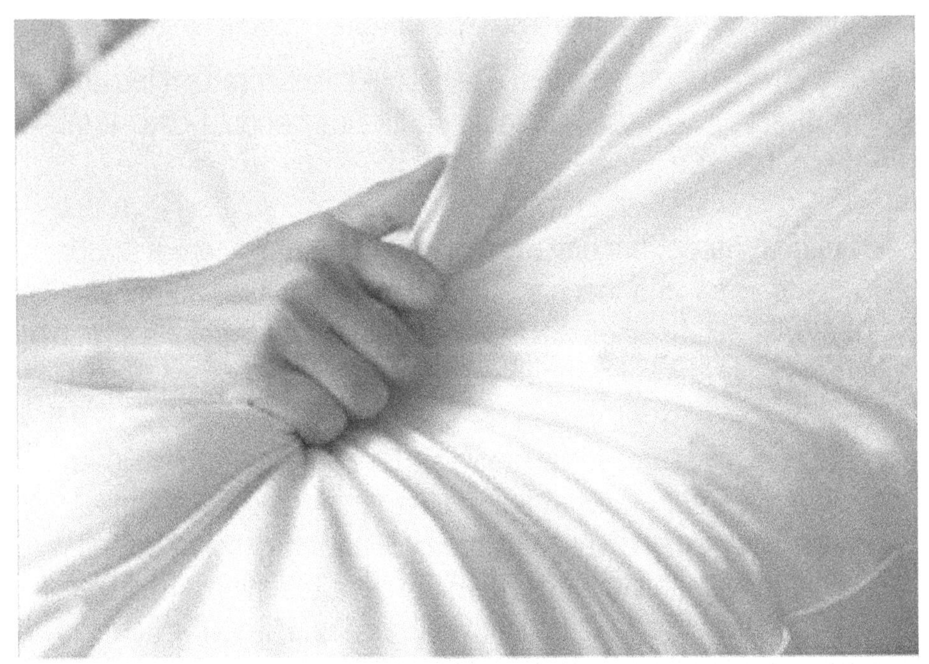

8

8

SEXUAL BEHAVIOUR AND CHILDREN

And it came to pass after these things, that his master's wife cast her eyes upon Joseph and she said. Lie with me.
- Genesis 39:7

Children develop sexually, just as they develop physically, emotionally and socially. Even young children have sexual feeling and may engage in sexual behavior if not careful.

It can be easy for parents to talk with their children about the differences between right and wrong, but it is often more difficult for parents to talk with their children about sexual development.

At a very young age, children begin to explore their bodies so as children grow older, they will need guidance in learning about these body parts and their functions.

BODY SAFETY TEACHING TIPS FOR PARENTS

Use appropriate language.

Teach children proper names for all body parts, including names such as genitals, penis, vagina, breasts, buttocks and private parts. Making up names for body parts may give the idea that there is something bad about the proper name.

Understand why your child has a special name for the body part but teach the proper name, too. Also, teach your child which parts are private (parts covered by a swimming suit).

Evaluate your family's respect for modesty

While modesty isn't a concept most young children can fully grasp, you can still use this age to lay a foundation for future.

DISCUSSIONS AND MODEL GOOD BEHAVIOR

If you have children of various ages, for example, it's important to teach your younger children to give older siblings their privacy. Usually, older siblings will teach the younger ones to get their clothes on, for example, because they might have friends over or because they are maturing and feel modest even in front of their younger brothers and sisters.

Do not force affection.

Do not force your children to give hugs or kisses to people they do not want to. It is their right to tell even grandma or grandpa that they do not want to give them a kiss or a hug goodbye.

Inappropriate touching- especially by a trusted adult- can be very confusing to a child. Constantly reinforce the idea that their body is their own, and they can protect it. It is very important that your child knows he or she has to tell you or another trusted grown-up if they have been touched. That way, your child knows it's also your job to protect them.

***Explain what a Good vs Bad Touches are*.**

You can explain a "good touch" as a way for people to show they care for each other and help each other (hugging, holding hands, changing a baby's diaper).

A "bad touch" is the kind you do not like and want it to stop right away, (i.e., hitting, kicking, or touching private parts). Reassure your child that most touches, but that they should say "NO" and need to tell you about any touches that are confusing or that scare them.

Give your Children a Solid Rule.

Teach them it is NOT okay for anyone to look at or touch their private parts, or what is covered by their swimsuits. It is easier for a child to follow a rule and they will more immediately recognize a "bad touch" if they have this guideline in mind. Reassure your children that you will listen to them, believe them, and want to keep them protected.

***Control Media Exposure*.**

Get to know the rating systems of video games, movies and television shows and make use of the parental controls available through many internet, cable, and satellite providers. Providing appropriate alternatives is an important part of avoiding exposure to sexual content in the media. Be aware that children may see adult sexual behaviors in person or on screens and may not tell you that this has occurred.

Review this Information Regularly with your Children.

Some good times to talk to your children about personal safety are during bath time, bedtime, and before any new situation. From child care to sports practices to dance classes, music classes not to mention camps and after school programs, children are meeting and interacting with many different adults and children on a daily basis.

Expect Questions.

The questions your child asks and the answers that are appropriate to give will depend on your child's age and ability to understand. The following tips might make it easier for both of you:

1. Don't laugh or giggle, even if the question is cute.
   Don't react with anger.
   Your child shouldn't be made to feel ashamed for his or her curiosity
2. Be brief, Don't go into a long explanation. Answer in simple terms. For example, your preschooler doesn't need to know the details of intercourse
3. See if your child wants or needs to know more.
   Follow up your answer with, does that answer your question?

4. Listen to your child's responses and reactions.
5. Be prepared to repeat yourself.

What is trending today is spirit of seduction that is attacking our children character and scattering their sense of vision and discarded their future dream.

Our children are being seduce and as a result of this, some hero and champions destinies are being truncated in our society.

Sexual activation when you are not married reduce or stopped greatness in a child's life. The children that God has given for Sign and Wonders in this generation meanwhile resulting from disobedience to God's rule about sex.

Parents must train up their children to obey God's rule about sex because this is the crucial part of their life.

The danger with "come to bed with me without control" Self Control like Joseph is needed.

Power and Control

A need for power and control often contribute to misbehavior. Sometimes defiant and argumentative behavior results when a child attempts to assert control.

When behavior problems result from a child's attempt to have control over a situation, a power struggle may ensue. One way to avoid this is to offer a child two choices. For example, ask "Would you rather clean your room now or after this TV show is over?" This can reduce a lot of arguments and increase the likelihood that a child will comply with instructions.

HOW PARENTS SHOULD DEAL WITH PROBLEMATIC BEHAVIOUR IN THEIR CHILDREN.

Bad behavior is often a sign that children are stressed and punishment isn't the best solution.

"For a man to conquer himself is the first and noblest of all victories." Thus wrote the philosopher Plato in the 4th century BC, thereby instilling the idea that character is built upon self-control.

Children who are in a heightened state of emotional arousal can have very sensitive limbic systems, where their brains are primed to respond to threats even when none exist. For example, experiments have shown that children who are chronically over-aroused will label neutral faces as hostile.

This means that children who react with hostility or by shutting down are likely showing the outward signs of an inward experience of stress overload. If we don't recognize the signs, figure out what is stressing them, and help them to cope instead of using blame, threats, or punishments—we will continue to make matters worse for them, rather than better.

A parent's reaction to a child's stress is important to their later ability to self-regulate, starting in the first years of their life.

Nature intends for human parents to play a close, nurturing role with their offspring and to take advantage of the "interbrain" the shared intuitive channel of communication between a parent and child that is maintained by touch, shared gaze, voice, and, most of all, shared emotion. This is what helps a stressed child develop a way of self-soothing that will stay with them and allow them to cope with stressors in their lives.

Providing warm, nurturing care early in life can go a long way toward stress management. But that doesn't mean that parents are solely responsible for their child's ability to adapt. Even kids who have enjoyed warm nurturing parenting can have trouble with self-regulation. That's why it's important to understand how it works and how we parent can help

1. **Recognize when your Children are Over-stressed**

A lot of your work as a parent involves learning how to understand the meaning of behaviors that you would otherwise find troubling or irritating. If you learn to read the signs and recognize them for what they are—a signal of a system on overload—you will be able to resist assigning blame or labels to your children. Reframing your children's behavior as a reaction to stress rather than willful misbehavior, and learning to listen to your children and to observe them with curiosity, is the first and perhaps most important step in self-regulation.

2. **Identify the Stressors in your Children's Lives**

Stress in children often involves disappointments in their relationships, schoolwork, and other purposeful activities, or having too much to do in too little time. But stress can also be hidden and have biological sources. For example, some children are highly distressed by too much noise, light, or odor, and this can cause ongoing problems in their lives that may be hidden from you. They may also find boredom, waiting, or sitting still extremely stressful. Stressors can come from many sources biological, emotional, cognitive, and social domains so it's important to consider all of these.

Though our environment may be highly stressful to our children, we often overlook information that could alert us to this fact. We or they may carry on as if it doesn't matter. That doesn't mean that their unconscious mind isn't registering the stress and responding with stress, though, which can in turn create a fight, flight, or freeze response.

Parents can look for patterns of behavior such as children always breaking down around 5:30 pm to help figure out what their children's stressors are perhaps they are hungry at that hour. Or, if it's less obvious, try reviewing in your head the different domains of their lives and what might be causing stress. Whatever you do, don't become a further drain on them by reacting in anger or judgment. Instead, try to listen and calmly affirm what seems to be going on for your children.

3. **Reduce those Stressors**

It's amazing how simply reducing sources of stress can change a child's behavior quickly. I once saw a child who was sensitive to noise, light, and textures labeled as a "problem child" by his teacher, only to have that opinion completely reversed when she realized that dimming the classroom lights changed his demeanor drastically. Sadly, the child had had to endure her judgment, communicated through raised voices and hardened facial expressions, for some time prior. In fact, she'd also labeled his father and grandfather as difficult.

The same thing can happen to parents who don't pay attention to what stresses their children and bring it into their conscious awareness. Once sources of stress have been identified, it's much easier to either help our kids avoid them or to mitigate them, as best we can perhaps by moving our dinner hour earlier or dimming the lights or giving them a hug after they've failed a test.

Sometimes, reducing our children's stress involves understanding what stresses us out and how it impacts our behavior. Learning how to soothe our own stress can help us self-regulate our emotions and lead to less reactivity toward our kids when they are suffering, as well as provide important role modelling for them.

4. **Help your Children Find Calming Strategies that Work for them**

We all need strategies for reducing tension and replenishing our energy. No one size fits all, so it's important to read the signs in your children, recognize their unique sources of stress, and make sure their self-regulation strategies fit their needs.

Mindfulness has been touted as a way to instill calm energy and to make our children more aware. But sometimes our children can get so used to feeling excessive stress that a state of hyper-alertness becomes “normal,” so much so that sitting still and focusing on their breathing a typical mindfulness exercise can be a thousand times more distressing than being manic.

Helping your children to slowly develop an awareness of their inner states and to find relaxation techniques that help them calm down can be incredibly empowering. Teaching your children mindful breathing if done slowly and with supports in place can be one technique to help them increase awareness of their need for calm.

But it's important that calming techniques are experienced by your children as enjoyable, too, and don't add to their stress inadvertently. There are many relaxation exercises that produce calm, such as practicing yoga, taking a walk, or working on art projects, for example. Encourage your children to experiment with what helps them most and support them in finding relief.

5. **Take a Long-term Perspective**

When you help your children find self-regulation strategies, be careful to consider the distinction between "quiet" and "calm." For example, a child may be quiet when playing video games, but no one would mistake that for calm, and you shouldn't either. Their brains are producing stress hormones galore when they are engaged and quiet playing video games. The point of finding strategies is not to make your life easier in the short run (by having your kids remain quiet), but to make their life easier and more productive in the long run (by helping them handle stress in a calming manner).

Of course, following my advice doesn't mean that your children will never misbehave, or that all of their problematic behaviors are a response to stress. But, so much of the time, misbehavior is a cry for help a cry that we, as parents and adults, need to answer with compassion and understanding, not punishment. Following the steps of self-regulation does not guarantee your child will suddenly stop irritating or frustrating you, but it may help prevent some unnecessary suffering. Our research has shown that following these steps is a powerful way for children to change their behavior. When your children see that you truly understand them and that you are committed to doing what you can to help, it will go a long way toward improving your relationship with them, as well as their ability to cope with life's challenges.

And that will reduce everyone's stress

TIPS TO UNDERSTAND YOUR CHILD PSYCHOLOGY

Realizing and accepting your child's likes, dislikes, qualities (good or bad) is the key to being a good parent. When you accept them just the way they are, they get a sense of security. Here are a few tips to help you understand your child:

1. ***Observe***

   You need to know your child if you want to understand him. It is possible to do so simply by being around him and observing him. When you see him playing, asking for a certain thing, reacting in a certain manner to situations, his interaction with others, etc., you get to know a great deal about his overall personality.

2. ***Be your Child's Best Friend***

   Making your child realize that you are always there for him whenever he needs you can be your first step towards attaining this goal. This will make him feel secure, loved and wanted. Help him to open up to you.

3. ***Spend Quality Time with your Child***

   Being around your child isn't enough. To know him better do activities together like playing games, cooking (children are always eager to help), cleaning up cupboards or his room, etc.

4. ***Praise your Child***

   Praising him for good work done will boost his self-esteem. However, overpraise can make him arrogant and snobbish.

5. **Listen**

ByListening to your Child, you get to know him more. Doing so will make him feel that you are interested in his life. This will in turn help to strengthen the bond between you two.

6. **Talking**

Talking to your child that are of interest to him could help him open up to you. In this way, you could initiate conversations more easily and get to know your child better.

7. **Give Full Attention while Talking**

Always maintain eye contact while talking to your child. By doing so, you will make sure your child believes that you are listening and what he is saying is of utmost importance to you.

8. **Give Respec**t

When your child talks about any of his insecurities, fears, or any situation where he has been put to shame, do not laugh or ridicule him. You need to understand that for a child (especially during his adolescent years), it isn't particularly easy to open up. It must have taken a lot of courage on his part to do so.

9. **Explaining**

Children up to the age of 5 – 6 will abide by all the rules created by you or the decisions you have taken for their betterment. The real problem lies with adolescents. Blame it on their age. In such situations just try and explain as to why you had to take a certain decision or do a certain thing. At that moment they may be angry with you, but eventually, with time, they will understand.

10. **Taking Opinion**

Ask for his opinion where it is necessary. Doing so will make him feel important and will raise his self-worth

11. Discovering the Reasons Behind His Behaviour

If your child has been misbehaving or has shown some negative behaviour, try to find out the cause behind it. By doing so, you will find out where you have been going wrong as a parent, and it will give you a chance to enhance your parenting skills.

12. **Knowing their Likes and Dislikes**

Knowledge about what your child likes, and dislikes will also help you know them better.

13. **Freedom of Expression**

Allow your child to express himself the way he wants to. You could get a glimpse of how he thinks or what he wants.

14. **Don't be Too Curious**

Every parent is eager to know what is happening in their child's life especially in case your child is an adolescent but don't be overly curious. Too much curiosity on your part could make him feel that you don't believe in him and this could end the bond between the two of you.

15. **Think Like Them**
    It is important to think like them while talking to them or doing an activity together. This will give him a sense of familiarity.

16. **Let their Imagination Take Wings**
    While taking a stroll with your little one, observe him. He may see something quite different to what you are seeing. Do not stop him when he does so. This will help you get an insight into his inner world.

HOW TO DEAL WITH TANTRUMS

The Challenge

Your two-year old child launches into a fit of screaming, when he is upset. He stomps and thrashes about. The parent then wonders: 'Is my child normal? Does he throw tantrums because of something I am doing wrong? Will he ever grow out of this? You can help your two-year-old to change his behavior. First, though, consider what could be contributing to it.

Why it happens?

Small children have limited experience in handling their emotions. That factor alone can lead to an occasional tantrum. But there is more. Think about the change that a child experiences at about age two. From the time that he was born, his parents catered to his every need. If he cried, for example, they came running. 'Is the baby sick? Does he need to be fed? Soothed? Changed?' The parents did whatever was needed to make things better. And that was proper because a baby is fully dependent upon his parents. At about age two, however, a child begins to realize that his parents are catering for him less and less. In fact, instead of their serving his needs, they expect him to comply with their wishes.

The tables have turned, and a two-year-old may not take well to the change without protest—perhaps in the form of a tantrum. In time, a child usually adjusts to the fact that his parents are his instructors, not just his caretakers. Hopefully, he also comes to see that his role is to be obedient to [his] parents. In the meantime, a child may test every fiber of his parents' patience with one tantrum after another.

What Can You Do?

Be understanding. Your child is not a miniature adult. Having little experience in dealing with his emotions, he may overreact when he is upset. Try to see the situation through his eyes. Bible principle: 1 Corinthians 13:11.

Stay calm. When your child is having a tantrum, losing your temper will not help. To the extent possible, ignore the tantrum and react matter-of-factly. Remembering why tantrums occur will help you to stay calm. Bible principle: Proverbs 19:11.

Hold your ground. If you give in to whatever it is your child is demanding, he will likely throw another tantrum the next time he wants something. Calmly show your child that you mean what you say.

Bible principle:
Matthew 5:37.

Be patient. Do not expect tantrums to disappear overnight, especially if you have given your child reason to believe that his behavior will sway you. If you react properly and consistently, however, the tantrums will likely diminish. Eventually, they will stop altogether. The Bible says that love is patient. 1Corinthians 13:4.

As a parent, also try the following: When the tantrum begins, hold your child in your arms (if possible) and, without hurting him, restrict him from thrashing about. Do not shout at your child. Just wait for the storm to pass. Eventually, the child will realize that the tantrum has got him nowhere. Designate an area where you can put your child when he has a tantrum. Tell him that he may come out when he has calmed down, and then leave him there. If your child has a tantrum in public, remove him from the view of others. Do not give in just because he is making a spectacle. That will only leave your child with the message that by throwing a tantrum, he can get whatever he wants.

SOCIAL MEDIA, CHILDREN AND PARENTS

Social media is a great online learning platform to reach children and also the fastest way to evangelized to children of this generation.

Everyone's life is changing because of the evaluation of social media. The benefits of using social media in children and homes cannot be over emphasized. It offers more opportunities to share knowledge and experience in a fun and exciting way. Most of the children we plan to reach are on one social media platform so we can reach a wide verity of them using social media.

WHAT IS SOCIAL MEDIA?

Social media is a computer based technology that facilitates the sharing of ideas, thoughts and information through the building of virtual network and communities, social media is internet based and gives users quick electronic communication and content.

WHY SOCIAL MEDIA FOR CHILDREN?

1. **Contents are saved and can be revisited**

   Contents that are posted on social media platforms are saved unless the account or video is deleted, this gives room for the message to be revisited and referred to thereby creating a catalogue of lessons and messages for children to have.

2. **Social Media as a Communication Channel**

   Effective communication plays a major role between the parent, teacher and child. If proper communication is not available, both teaching and learning will become difficult. With the help of the internet, children get connected with friends, peers, family and teachers too. It makes the child become active participants rather than passive consumers of content.

3. **Social Media as an Engagement Tool**
   Social media tools can be used to increase children's engagement. Social media has grabbed the attention of millions of people across the world; the same thing can be used to draw the attention of children to the learning opportunities provided the teacher. Both the children, teacher and parent can share their ideas on social media.

4. **Experience Global Exposure**
   Social media allows for interactionwith people across the world, the teacher can get immense knowledge from it. They get to know about diverse culture present in the world. It includes their culture, traditions, language, lifestyle, food, habits, etc.

5. **Social Media as a Collaborative Platform**
   Another vital benefit of social media is collaboration. Through collaboration, you can work together intellectually and socially to achieve a common goal with the children and other children teachers. Teachers can use social media to gather and share information from both internal and external resources. You can generate your own learning contents too.

5. **Social Media as a Research Tool**
   Any teacher can quickly and easily find high authority research material using social media in education. You can research on online to find relevant material on any topic related to your class. You can join various educational groups online too.

7. **Helps to Gain Wider Knowledge**
   Social media aids the teacher to gain more knowledge through data and information gathering. Whenever teachers encounter a problem they go through various online platform to collect information to help solve their problem.

SOCIAL MEDIA PLATFORMS FOR CHILDREN, TEACHERS AND PARENTS

YouTube:

This is an online platform for sharing videos it was created in 2005 YouTube allows the users to upload, view, rate, report and comment on videos, contents available are video clips, TV shows clips, most content on YouTube is uploaded by individuals, to upload on this platform registration is needed after that you upload an unlimited number of videos. As at 2019 more than 500 hours of content uploaded to YouTube every minute and one billion hours of contents being watched on YouTube every day, YouTube currently has about 1.9billion users.

Instagram:
This is photo and video sharing networking service it was originally launched in October 2010 on IOS the android version was launched in April 2012, Users can upload pictures and videos that can be viewed by other users currently there are about one billion users.

WhatsApp:
This is a platform for text messaging voice messages, making voice and videos calls, sharing images, documents, and other media, WhatsApp basically runs on mobile devices but can be accessible from computers in 2015 WhatsApp became the most popular messaging app in the world and has about two billion users.

Zoom:
This is video telephony software program, the free version provides a wide chatting service that allows up to 100 devices at once with a 40 minutes' time restriction for free accounts having meeting of three or more participants, users have the option of upgrading by subscribing to one of the plans available with the highest allowing up to a thousand participants with no time restriction.

Facebook:
This is a social media and social networking service it was launched in 2004, Facebook can be accessed from any devicewith internet connectivity, after registering
Users can create profiles and post information about

themselves they can also post texts photos and multimedia and share it with whoever is on their friend list Facebook has about 2.70 billion monthly users.

Pinterest:

This is an image shearing and social media service designed to enable saving discovery of information, the creators of Pinterest summarized the service as a catalogue of ideas.

Mixlr:

This is an audio streaming service platform that allows the users to be spontaneous, live audio can be broadcasted any input device can be connected sounds can be added to your playlist, sessions can be record on the move you can chat and engage with your listeners and messages and can be recorded offline and later uploaded.

SOCIAL MEDIA STRATEGY

1. **Determine your Target Audience and Platform**

   Ask yourself, who are you trying to reach and where are they gathering online? The social media platform you decide to start with should always be determined by your target audience. If you are trying to reach children of different age groups, you might find they are likely not congregating in the same digital spaces consistently. If you are not sure where to begin, a good rule of thumb might be to start with Facebook, which is still one of the most used social media platforms, ranking in second after YouTube, according to Pew Research.

2. **Create a daily posting strategy**
   Ask yourself, "What exactly are you going to post and when? If you want to stay in front of your audience and increase the likelihood of engagement, you might consider posting every day. If this idea intimidates you, no worries – there are number of handy social media schedulers that will do the heavy lifting for you. Most scheduling tools like Buffer and have free plans that allow you to connect to and schedule posts across multiple social networks. If set up well, these tools have the potential of saving you hours of work! But posting daily won't have nearly as much of an impact if you are not strategic about the kind of content you are posting. Not only should you post content that is fresh and engaging, but also consider posting specific content on certain days to give your audience an element of unpredictable predictability".

Social can Change

Social Media can change your children's ministry by helping you to develop a powerful network of people who share a common passion and interest. These fellow labourers are people who can help you to grow in your ability to minister to children. They can provide accountability in peer-to-peer relationships and they can give much needed encouragement when things are not going well.

REFERENCES

1. Application Study Bible, New King James Version
2. Anointed Destiny: Changing Prayers for your Children., MFM, Onike Lagos
3.· Sexual Behaviors in young Children., American Academy of Pediatrics, copyright 2021
4· Children Evangelism Ministry, Lagos Nigeria.,
5. Awake July, 2013 pp4-5
6. How to spend more Quality time with your Child? by Harley A. Rotbert, M.D feb. 2012
7. Parenting is not a competitive., Sport., Kristen Hewitt
8.· How to set Healthy boundaries with your Child., by Debbie Princus, MS LMHC
9. Children Misbehavior Project.. by Temitope Okosodo
10. Responsive Parenting, principles for Raising Connected. Boyd., by D. Brooks PsyD,LPC 2018
11. The Rules of Parenting by Richard Templar 2008
12. Senior lecturer, Faculty of Education, University, Malaysia by Dr. ZuwatiHasim
13.· Why Nagging Doesn't Work and Can Be Detrimental by KidsMckenna Meyers
14. How consistency Improves kids' Behavior by Michael Grose
15. Parenting, Better Parenting By Brandie Weikle
16. Parenting/Discipline By Jonathan Stern
17. New Strait TimesNews PaperThursday, 7 January 2021, 9:55am
18. Psychologist and teacher By Dr. Jan Philamon

www.ingramcontent.com/pod-product-compliance
Ingram Content Group UK Ltd.
Pitfield, Milton Keynes, MK11 3LW, UK
UKHW021917190726
13853UKWH00002B/712

9 789789 898619